California's
Old Missions

A Bicentennial Book

California's Old Missions

THE STORY OF THE FOUNDING OF THE 21 FRANCISCAN MISSIONS IN SPANISH ALTA CALIFORNIA 1769-1823

By
Paul H. Kocher

FRANCISCAN HERALD PRESS

1434 WEST 51st STREET • CHICAGO, 60609

A BICENTENNIAL BOOK

California's Old Missions: The Story of the Founding of the 21 Franciscan Missions in Spanish Alta California, 1769-1823 by Paul H. Kocher, Professor Emeritus, Stanford University. Copyright © 1976, Franciscan Herald Press, 1434 West 51st St., Chicago, Illinois 60609.

Library of Congress Cataloging in Publication Data
Kocher, Paul H.
  California's old missions.

  At head of title: A bicentennial book.
  Bibliography: x + 178 pages
  Includes index
  1. Spanish missions of California. 2. Franciscans
in California. 3. Franciscans — Missions. 4. Missions —
California. 5. California — History — To 1846. I. Title.
F864.K62   266'.2'09794   76-2699
ISBN 0-8199-0601-8

MADE IN THE UNITED STATES OF AMERICA

COMMEMORATING THE BICENTENNIAL
OF THE FOUNDING OF THE UNITED STATES AND
OF THE FOUNDING OF THE SIXTH AND THE SEVENTH
OF CALIFORNIA'S OLD MISSIONS,
THE MISSION OF SAN FRANCISCO AND
THE MISSION OF SAN JUAN CAPISTRANO,
BY THE SAINTLY FR. JUNÍPERO SERRA,
THE FATHER OF CALIFORNIA

Foreword

While the Liberty Bell rang out in Philadelphia in 1776, the mission bells were ringing for the first time in San Francisco in that same year. By 1776 Fray Junípero Serra, accompanying the military expedition under Gov. Portolá, had founded seven missions — San Diego (1769), San Carlos Borromeo or Carmel (1770), San Antonio (1771), San Gabriel (1771), San Luis Obispo (1772), San Juan Capistrano (1776), and San Francisco or Dolores (1776).

Fray Junípero Serra would found two more; his friar followers would complete the string of 21 missions forming an irregular line reaching from San Diego to Sonoma, and connected by El Camino Real (The King's Highway).

Today the modern highway along the coast of California, U.S. 101, follows so closely the course of the road established by the pioneers two hundred years ago that one can easily say that one is walking in the footsteps of Fray Junípero Serra and his companions.

Nor were these missions an innovation of the Spanish pioneers. They were actually the "new" and the very last missions in our Spanish Borderlands.

Why another book on the California Missions when there have been so many already? This book has a unique approach and is a very worth while contribution to the celebration of the Bicentennial of our country. It tells the story of the "founding" of the missions with the problems and the hardships entailed — an impartial account that is fair to everyone concerned. But Appendix I also has an entire history of each mission briefly summarized, thus giving the reader a correct overview of the development and subsequent fate of the missions.

A double series of paintings and photographs of all 21 missions shows them as they looked in 1903 when they were published in the *San Francisco Chronicle* and a modern series photographed in 1975 by Ed Kumler.

For the 1903 pictures of the missions we are indebted to the Historical Museum of Mission San Luis Obispo, where they are displayed. We are deeply thankful to Leonard Mayta for the prints of them used in this book.

Dr. Paul H. Kocher is Emeritus Professor of English and Humanities, Stanford University. Since retiring in 1971, he has written a history of Mission San Luis Obispo (1772-1972) for this mission's bicentennial. Other books by Dr. Kocher are *Science and Religion in Elizabethan England,* Huntington Library, and *Master of Middle-Earth: the Fiction of J. R. Tolkien,* Houghton Mifflin Company.

In this journey through the 21 missions, discover how these hard-headed friars with the soft hearts of sanctity, in sheltering and educating their converts, created in simplicity and strength a type of architecture which considered from the standpoint of practical living, climatic background, materials of construction, and ethnic significance, has rarely been equalled in any land. It is a matchless heritage they have left us!

— The Publisher

Contents

Illustrations

1/Before 1769

More than two centuries before the first California mission was even dreamed of there began a long series of shipboard explorations of the region's west coast. These started the process of mapping and naming some of its chief harbors, capes, rivers, and islands, not without some misleading errors which were to confuse the land expeditions founding the missions in years to come.

By custom the military leader of every Spanish exploring party in the New World had at his side from the beginning one or more priests to act as chaplains. Their function was not exclusively religious, however. Whether on ship or on land they were expected to keep a written record describing the events of each day and the character of the region traversed. If the territory had never been explored before, these priestly geographers also named the principal landmarks which caught their eye, and ended the day by giving the evening campsite the name of the saint whose feast-day fell on the following day. Since each day of the year was the feast-day of several saints, the chronicler usually selected a saint who had been a member of his Order, if he happened to be a friar or monk, and, if not, then some saint whose life seemed particularly suited to the situation of the explorers at the time. To remind him of the dates of the various feast-days every priest carried with him on his person an *Ordo*

1

or *Calendar* for each year listing this and other information necessary to the celebration of Mass on any given day.[1]

Other members of the expedition usually deferred to the choice of names made by the priestly scribe. But the military commander might intervene to call some major feature after the Spanish king or his viceroy in Mexico City. And, as the priest was well aware, the common soldiers were also busy every day identifying various spots along the way with titles reminding them of some striking incident or other which happened during the day. Perhaps a sword had been stolen by an Indian, or a lame chief had danced, or an unusual seabird had been shot, or a bear hunted, or a sack of flour had fallen into a river being crossed, and so on. Any or all of these might be memorialized by descriptive words which became place-names. When that happened the diarist faithfully noted them in his records next to the saint's name he himself had conferred.

At the end of the exploration, copies of the diary were always sent to the priest's religious superiors and to the civil authorities in Mexico City for study. Along with this diary often went a map to aid in visualizing the route taken. If the findings were important, several copies might be circulated, and a few diaries even achieved print. In any case they were readily available for study by later explorers.

The earliest predecessor of the California missionaries, Juan Rodríguez Cabrillo,[2] sailing up the coast with two tiny ships, reached what is now called San Diego on September 28, 1542. Since the feast day of the Archangel Michael fell on September 29, he called the port San Miguel, and later gave the name Galera (seagull) to the cape we know as Point Concepción. Soon afterwards the annual Spanish Philippine galleon established its route to Mexico along the great circle: from Manila northeast to Japan, then eastward to the California coast, then south along the coast to Acapulco.

The galleon's need during its six-month voyage for an intermediate stop in some harbor along the more northerly reaches of that coast was later to stimulate a search which culminated in Spanish discovery and occupation of the port of Monterey—none too suitable a port, as it turned out. In the meantime the pilot and sailors of the galleon were becoming well acquainted with the California coast visible from the sea. But they seem never to have noticed the entrance to what is now San Francisco Bay. Late in 1595, a pilot named Sebastian Rodríguez Cermeño anchored in what we now call Drake's Bay, but which he called "La Baya de San Francisco."[3] The name stuck for over a century and a half, mystifying Spanish land expeditions, from 1769 on for several years, as to the nature of the great inland Sea which they could not cross in trying to reach what they thought was La Baya de San Francisco.

After Cabrillo came Sebastián Vizcaíno with three ships, under instruction to survey the west coast as far northwards as possible but not to change the names of landmarks already appearing on the maps. Nevertheless, when Vizcaíno entered the port of Cabrillo's San Miguel on November 10, 1602, he renamed it San Diego de Alcalá because he went ashore on November 12, the eve of San Diego's feast day. This change of nomenclature may well have been suggested by the three Carmelite friars aboard Vizcaíno's ships, particularly Fr. Ascención, who was the official diarist of the expedition. In this way the first of Fr. Serra's Alta California missions, later erected at this port in 1769, came to be given to the patronage of San Diego.

Similarly, the Channel island Vizcaíno reached on November 25, feast day of St. Catherine of Alexandria, Roman virgin and martyr, acquired her name in its Spanish form, Santa Catalina. On December 4 the Vizcaíno friars christened the Channel itself after Santa Barbara, another early virgin-martyr, whose feast-day that was. As they sailed northward along the coast in plain view of the coast range they decided, on December 13, feast day of Santa Lucía (St. Lucy, died c. 304), yet another virgin-martyr, to honor the mountains with her name. These Carmelite friars seem to have preferred the names of early virgin-martyrs. But just south of Monterey they called the river valley there Carmelo after their own Order (Mount Carmel) in the Holy Land.

Monterey itself, reached on December 16, 1602, the friars had no part in naming. Vizcaíno as captain intervened to call it Monterey after the then viceroy of New Spain, Gaspar de Zúñiga, Conde de Monte Rey. But Vizcaíno was so over-enthusiastic in his praise of the harbor as being excellently protected from ocean winds that he confused Portolá's expedition of 1769 into doubting that the exposed bay they saw could possibly be the port Vizcaíno admired. Since accounts of Vizcaíno's voyage seem to have been widely read in Mexico City, his names for many features of the Alta California coast became accepted by everyone, including Portolá and his men.

Also highly influential was a book entitled *Navegación Especulativa y Practica* published in Manila in 1734 by Joseph González Cabrero Bueno, chief pilot of the Philippine galleons.[4] He had been observing the California coast from the sea for many years as the galleons sailed south along it. Cabrero Bueno, as he was usually called, described not only the Monterey region but also Cermeño's Baya de San Francisco farther north. His influence, combined with that of Vizcaíno, fixed in the minds of the planners in Mexico City the conviction that the prime targets for exploration and occupation along the Alta California seacoast should be first San Diego, then Monterey, and then the so-called Bay of San Francisco, in that order. This idea governed the thinking of both Viceroy Carlos de Croix and Visitador

Joseph de Gálvez when they were planning the great Spanish expansion into Alta California in the 1760's. Furthermore, they believed that where the military presidios were, there also should be the missions to convert and pacify the Indian natives. So the locations and, in part, the names of three missions were determined before the 1769 expedition got under way. Unhappily that expedition also had derived from previous voyagers serious misconceptions about Monterey Bay, as well as a total ignorance that the present San Francisco Bay even existed.

But what religious Order was to supply the chaplains for the explorers of Alta California, and subsequently the missionaries for its missions? Not the Jesuits, for in 1767 they had been summarily expelled by the Spanish king from the whole of the New World under an unlikely charge of treason to the crown. Their expulsion immediately put a heavy drain upon the other Orders in Mexico to provide priests to man the very numerous abandoned Jesuit missions. When Gálvez and De Croix had to decide which Order to choose for the advance into Alta California, they could have fixed upon the Dominicans, the Augustinians, the Carmelites or many others who had houses in Mexico City. Just what factors made them select the Franciscans is hard to say with any certainty. But the fact that this Order had three large colleges in Mexico—San Fernando, Queretaro, and Zacatecas—no doubt carried weight. Also, Franciscans had been the principal missionaries for over two centuries in the northern part of New Spain or Mexico, including New Mexico, Arizona and Texas—all of it in fact, except those parts where the Jesuits had their missions. San Fernando College had been sustaining five missions in the Sierra Gorda for years with considerable success. And since 1750 this college had an impressive leader in Fr. Junípero Serra, who had not only served in the Sierra Gorda but also had become highly admired in the capital for his preaching and his extra-ordinary missionary zeal. Gálvez and De Croix may well have attended his Masses.

At least as early as September 24, 1768, Gálvez was writing letters to Fr. Serra outlining the plans for Franciscan missions in Alta California as if Fr. Serra's presidency over them had already been settled.[5] That letter of September 24 projects a minimum of three missions there, one at San Diego de Alcalá, one at Monterey, and a third dedicated to San Buenaventura somewhere between the other two. Soldier guards were to be encamped between these missions until a chain of missions "a day's journey apart" had been founded. The *mission* at Monterey, wrote Gálvez, was to have as its patron San Carlos Borromeo "in honor of Carlos III of Spain and Viceroy Carlos de Croix . . . " but the titular patron of the Monterey presidio *church* was to be San José (St. Joseph), patron of the whole California expedition and of Gálvez personally. All subsequent missions founded in Alta California were to be named "after Franciscan saints, since it was appropriate that the missions under a particular Order be dedicated to the Order's saints."

Fr. Serra had asked wistfully whether there was to be no mission named in honor of St. Francis himself, founder of his Order. Gálvez answered, "Let him (St. Francis) find the port bearing his name and he will have a mission there." This reply shows that Gálvez was already thinking ahead to Cabrero Bueno's port of San Francisco, well north of Monterey. That would be the appropriate location for a mission dedicated to that saint, he said, and the St. Francis mission should be the first one established after the missions at San Diego and Monterey.

Gálvez's letter indicates at least one respect in which the choice of Franciscans as explorers and missionaries was to have momentous results for the names of missions in Alta

California. The missions were to be called after Franciscan saints specifically. How much difference this principle made can be gauged by comparing Alta California mission names with those of Baja California, where all the missions had been first established by Jesuits. There the names of famous Jesuits like San Ignacio (St. Ignatius), San Borja (St. Borgia), and San Javier (St. Xavier) appear along with those of the Virgin and St. Joseph. Franciscan saints are not included.

Giving Alta California to the Franciscans as their missionary territory had the even more important long-term effect of establishing here the Franciscan mission system, which differed from that of other Orders. And this system, in turn, determined the sorts of localities suitable for missions of this type. The Franciscan method for missions had first been developed by the remarkable Fr. Pedro Pérez de Mezquía in his Texas missions early in the eighteenth century. It had been further tested and refined in the Sierra Gorda missions after 1744 and thereafter became the blueprint for all missions sponsored by the three Franciscan colleges of Mexico.[6]

One of the guiding conceptions of the Franciscan mission was that all natives who had accepted the Catholic faith, or were being instructed in its teachings, must agree to live close to the mission church and to become a self-supporting community in all possible activities, including especially farming and ranching, building, weaving of cloth, blacksmithing and so on. A small guard of soldiers should help prevent disorders inside the community or attacks from outside, but the final decisions about discipline must always rest with the padres, not the military. These padres were the teachers of their flocks not only in religion but in the skills necessary to the mission's economic life. Such teaching could not proceed successfully unless the mission was situated far enough from military presidios and the pueblos of civilian settlers. Otherwise, conflicts of interest would forever be arising when,

for instance, the pueblos wanted the mission Indians to perform cheap manual labor for them or when the presidios
ordered missionaries to act as their chaplains. Two juris-
dictions with different aims could not live side by side in
harmony for any length of time. As we shall see, the many
discords which arose between Frs. Serra and Lasuén as
presidents of the California missions, on the one hand, and
the successive governors of the province on the other, are
traceable largely to the Franciscans' defense of their conception of what a mission should be.

Obviously this conception could be realized, or approxi-
mated, only in certain types of locations. The missions must
be founded in places fairly remote yet not too remote, plent-
ifully supplied with water for drinking and irrigation, surrounded by large tracts of fertile land for farming and graz-
ing, with accessible trees for building-timber and firewood,
preferably also with some stone for foundations and adobe
for brick walls—in short, everything needed for a large civil
and religious community able to satisfy its own needs. Of
course, few localities were as ideal as all this, but unless
they met most of these requirements they were likely to be
passed over.

If the Franciscans of the College of San Fernando ever
had any doubts about the validity of their mission system,
they lost them during the years 1768 to 1773 when they
were assigned to take over the former Jesuit missions in Baja
California. There they found that each mission was ad-
mininistered by a soldier appointed by Governor Portolá,
to whom they had to apply for money, food, and every other
necessity of life. Besides, the Christian Indians did not live
at these missions but in their native villages, whence they had
to travel to the church to attend Mass. Only too often they
preferred not to make the trip, especially if the distance was
long. Consequently they were not being well educated in

religion, farming, or anything else.

At a personal conference with Gálvez late in 1768[7] Fr. Serra was able to persuade the Visitador that for the missionary enterprise in Alta California, which was to begin in the following year, the Franciscans would need priests and material resources on a very large scale. To provide the latter Gálvez himself toured the Baja California missions, shutting down several which were dying, consolidating others, and combing all of them for whatever he thought they could spare for the new enterprise. What he gleaned in this way he sent to the northern-most mission of the peninsula, San Fernando de Velicatá, closest to San Diego and designed to act as a depot for supplies which could easily be picked up by the Portolá land expedition on its way north through Baja California. After the success of Portolá's band in founding Monterey in June, 1770, Gálvez's thinking advanced another step. He recognized that the Franciscans would need all their friars, including those still manning 'the missions of Baja California, in the region about to be opened up in the north. So, by amicable arrangement between the Franciscans and Dominicans, the latter were given in 1773 all missions south of San Diego, while the Fernandinos were allotted all of California north of it. And great was the relief of the latter at being in a rich new region where they could start afresh with missions in the familiar Franciscan pattern.

Notes

1. For this information I am indebted to Fr. Maynard Geiger, O.F.M., Archivist at Mission Santa Barbara.

2. For a summary of the voyages of both Cabrillo (1542) and Vizcaíno (1602) see Robert Glass Cleland, *From Wilderness to Empire* (New York: Alfred Knopf, 1949), pp. 9–15 and 33–42. Also Fr. Zephyrin Engelhardt, O.F.M., *Missions and Missionaries of California* 2 vols, 2nd ed. (Mission Santa Barbara, 1930), I, 26–7; 51ff; and Alberta Denis, *Spanish Alta California* (New York: Macmillian, 1927), pp. 5–12, 25–37.

3. Denis, p. 23.

4. The effects of Cabrero Bueno's book may be gauged by the respectful allusions to it in Fr. Crespi's diary of the first Portolá land expedition. See Herbert Bolton ed., *Historical Memoirs of New California* 4 vols. (New York: Russell & Russell, 1966), II, 190, 213, 215, 217, 222. In the same volume see also allusions by Fr. Palóu, pp. 289, 355, narrating events immediately following this expedition. Costansó's *Diario,* ed. Ray Brandes (Hogarth Press, 1970), p. 94, shows the confusion caused by Cabrero Bueno's description of Monterey, which Costansó called "the only clue of the expedition."

5. Fr. Maynard Geiger, *Life and Times of Fr. Junípero Serra, O.F.M., (1713–84)* 2 vols. (Washington, D.C., 1959), I, 204.

6. Geiger I, 116.

7. Geiger I, 206ff. This meeting also established the custom, which became standard, that the Pious Fund should contribute 1000 pesos to the founding of each mission, and should also give a stipend to each of the friars in residence with which to buy religious goods for the mission church. The stipend was first set at 700 pesos but later reduced to 400 pesos. For a description of the Pious Fund see Chapter 10.

2/Portolá's Expedition (1769-70)

But to return to 1769, when the land and sea detachments of the Portolá expedition finally assembled at San Diego on July 1. Two land columns had struggled up through the parched deserts and mountains of Baja California; and two newly built packet ships, the *San Carlos* and the *San Antonio,* surviving storm and scurvy, lay at anchor in the harbor. Their crews, however, were too decimated and too ill to continue sailing up the coast in search of Monterey. Plainly that search would have to proceed solely by land. Portolá divided his forces accordingly, leaving a part behind to establish a presidio and a mission at San Diego, as well as a hospital for the sick. He himself led the able-bodied remainder northward by land on July 14.

Fr. Serra's lameness had handicapped him so severely on the overland journey to San Diego that he remained behind, reluctantly declaring himself unfit for another land march. His restless spirit, however, refused to be sick. On July 15, the day after Portolá left, he started to found a mission with the aid of Frs. Parron and Vizcaíno (not Sebastián) in the midst of the general encampment. From long experience Fr. Serra knew that this was not a favorable site for a mission, but at the moment he had no alternative. The three priests began by erecting a cross and building an altar inside a brushwood hut. On July 16 they said Mass and dedicated the mission to San Diego de Alcalá, as Gálvez had instructed.[1] It was fitting that the same saint who guarded the presidio and the harbor should be patron of the mission, too.

A more appropriate saint for the first Alta California mission would have been hard to find.[2] San Diego de Alcalá (1400-1463) had been a Spanish Franciscan lay brother who served as a humble doorkeeper in his Order's monastery on the Canary Islands, on the edge, as it were, of a New World soon to be discovered. He showed a genius for helping and converting the Island poor who thronged to its doors. The parallel between his work and that which the Franciscans were about to do for the Indians in unknown California was too close to be missed.

Portolá was well aware of the importance of making written records of every event of his march for perusal by the officials in Mexico City and in Madrid. He had with him a wide variety of diarists: Miguel Costansó, a skilled engineer and cosmographer; Lt. Pedro Fages, to give the soldier's point of view; and two Franciscans, Frs. Juan Crespi and Antonio Gómez, the former a close friend of Fr. Serra. Of these Fr. Crespi was to be by far the most influential in bestowing holy names, some of which became the names of California missions, and many others which are still in use today for towns, rivers, lakes, and other topographical features.

Fr. Crespi was indeed a prince of diarists. Beginning with the departure from San Diego on July 14 he hardly missed a day during the entire six months, ten days, of the expedition.[3] Of course he had a particularly keen eye for promising mission sites, and described some of their attractions in detail. Each evening he gave to the camping place and its environs the name of a saint, preferably Franciscan or Biblical, whose feast-day fell on the morrow. If sometimes

San Diego Mission (founded 1769), in 1903 (top), and in 1975 (bottom).

he postponed one of them for a few days past the feast-day, the explanation usually is that some other saint had the same feast-day on the calendar and took precedence. Fr. Crespi also noted conscientiously any name given by the soldiery to each locality to celebrate some notable incident of the day. Examples are La Carpintería, where the men watched some Chumash Indians building one of their remarkable canoes, or Los Pedernales for the rocky headland near Point Concepción where they picked up flints for their muskets. Consequently religious and secular names stood side by side in Fr. Crespi's diary, competing for survival. Either might win in a given locality, as a modern map of California test-ifies, being liberally sprinkled with both kinds.

The many scores of names of Franciscan saints and members of the Holy Family which Fr. Crespi spread up and down the California coast offered the viceroys in Mexico City a wide choice of patrons for the missions built in the years that followed. Out of the total of twenty-one missions eventually built between San Diego and Sonoma ten were named after Franciscan saints and Biblical characters honored in Fr. Crespi's diary. The following table lists these ten, together with the date of the diary entry and of the official feast-day for each.

Diary date	Name	Feast day
July 16	Triumph of the Holy Cross	September 14
July 18	San Juan Capistrano	March 28
July 24	San Francisco Solano	July 13
July 30	San Miguel Arcángel	September 29
August 9	Santa Clara	August 12
August 21	San Luis Obispo	August 19
August 24	San Luis Rey de Francia	August 25
August 27	Concepción de María Santísima (near Point Concepción)	Principal feast-day, August 15

August 28	San Juan Bautista	June 24
September 29	San Miguel Arcángel	September 29
October 18	Santa Cruz (Holy Cross)	September 14

Since the expedition reached San Francisco Bay late in October and returned to San Diego by the same route by which they had come, Fr. Crespi had no occasion to bestow any additional names of saints or holy mysteries on the way back. In the list just given several further considerations are to be kept in mind. Discrepancies between diary date and feast-days come in the months between November and the middle of July because in that interval the expedition was either not journeying at all or was merely traversing old ground. Also, rather than miss the opportunity of naming localities after revered saints like San Juan Capistrano and San Juan Bautista, Fr. Crespi ignored their feast-days and fitted them in wherever he thought best. Furthermore, of course, most of the missions which were to bear these ten names were not in fact founded on or near the spots which Fr. Crespi assigned to their patrons.

Only a close reading of his diary can reveal how much of his nomenclature never achieved common use, much less the patronage of a mission.[4] It would reveal also that as the expedition approached San Francisco Bay late in October he sometimes had recourse to saints of other Orders, particularly Dominicans, presumably as a friendly gesture since there was never any lack of Franciscans. But the disfavor into which the Jesuits had fallen prevented Fr. Crespi from including a single Jesuit.

Two incidents, however, establish the depth of his devotion to St. Francis of Assisi, if anybody doubts it. Passing through the area that is now Los Angeles on August 1, 1769, he celebrated what he described as "the jubilee of Our Lady of the Angels at Porciúncula." The present Los Angeles River he also named "Porciúncula" on August 2. As a good Franciscan he had in mind the little church outside Assisi which served as the headquarters of St. Francis and his followers, and which they called Porciúncula (small portion). Without knowing it Fr. Crespi was thereby providing a name for the city which would be founded at this place in 1781, under the full Spanish title of "Nuestra Señora La Reina de los Angeles de Porciúncula" (Our Lady Queen of the Angels at Portiúncula). The erosion of the years wore down this tribute to Mary simply to Los Angeles, transforming it into a tribute to the Angels. The Franciscan memento of Porciúncula likewise fell by the wayside.

The other occasion came on Sunday, September 17, 1769, when the Portolá party were lost, weary and sick in the Santa Lucia mountains while feeling their way from the impassable Pacific shoreline towards the interior Salinas Valley. Frs. Crespi and Gomez took heart from the fact that this was the anniversary of the day of "the Impression of the Stigmata of Our Seraphic Father San Francisco" on "Mount Alberene" (Mt. Alverna or La Verna) and from the implied parallel with their own present travails. The expedition camped that night in a valley where they met a small band of friendly Indians. Fr. Crespi named the campsite La Hoya de la Sierra de Santa Lucía. "La Hoya" here probably meant "the river valley," though it could also mean "la Jolla" (the jewel), which in Spanish had an identical pronunciation. Its significance for mission history is that when Fr. Serra set out to found Mission San Antonio de Padua in 1771 he went to what he thought was La Hoya, in recollection of Fr. Crespi's putting the Indians there under the protection of St. Francis, Fr. Serra intended to find a mission site somewhere nearby. Ironically, he seems to have missed La Hoya by many miles.

Engineer Miguel Costansó also kept a record of the first

Portolá expedition, which he wrote up and signed on October 24, 1770, after his return to Mexico City.[5] It was not a diary with mention of daily place names but an overall analytical commentary on the country and its Indian inhabitants, with particular attention to the reasons for the indecision about Monterey. Consequently it has little direct interest for mission history except in so far as it outlines Indian character and culture. By contrast, Captain Fages' *Historical, Political and Natural Description of California,* written in 1775, relied most of the time on Fr. Crespi's diary for its geographical descriptions and names, both religious and secular. The Fages treatise leaned more heavily than its source, however, towards the soldier-given names.[6] Also, as in his comments on the newly founded Mission San Gabriel, Fages showed that he held a very un-Franciscan view of the function of a mission.[7] He thought of missions chiefly as useful centers around which to build settlements of Spanish civilians guarded by military presidios. Where such settlements were dangerously far from each other in crowded Indian country "it would be very desirable to establish a few more missions with their corresponding presidios" as a method of "reducing" the native. A far cry from the Franciscan belief that the purpose of a mission was primarily to bring Christianity to such natives! Since Fages' outlook was to be shared by virtually all the Spanish governors of California with whom the Franciscans, especially Frs. Serra and Lasuén, had to deal, it is not surprising that friction became endemic between the two sides. The wonder is that so much was accomplished in spite of the rubs.

Fr. Pedro Font, chaplain of the second Anza expedition in 1776 exemplifies in his diary a more common type of reliance on previous diaries, including Fr. Crespi's of 1769-1770 and 1772.[8] When following Fr. Crespi's route between San Diego and Monterey he adopted all of Crespi's holy names.

Being a meticulously careful scribe, he probably had with him a copy of the 1769-1770 diary, or a map made from it. When he reached Monterey with Anza in March, 1776, he found time to copy "the map of the port of San Francisco, which my cousin, Fr. Pablo Font, made in Mexico from the data in the diary kept by Fr. Juan Crespi in that journey which he made with Captain Fages"[9] to San Francisco in March, 1772. That the original map was drawn in Mexico from one of Fr. Crespi's diaries and then became available for copying in Monterey gives some idea how these documents circulated. By the time he reached San Francisco Bay on March 27 Fr. Font mentions having with him, in addition to the foregoing map, also "the diaries of Fr. Crespi and Fr. Palóu, kept by them in their journeys. . . ."[10] In fact, Fr. Font consulted these guides so constantly that he annoyed Anza, who remarked that he was exploring only for a presidio site, not for mission sites, with which the priests' diaries were heavily preoccupied.

Nevertheless, Fr. Font knew what he was doing. His record of Anza's planting a flag for a presidio on the north shore of the peninsula led Lt. Moraga later to the same spot in order to erect a fortification there. Fr. Font's entry in his journal on March 29 describing a beautiful river a short distance to the east which, "because it was Friday of Sorrows, we called the Arroyo de los Dolores,"[11] and which he judged highly suitable for one of the two missions planned for the San Francisco area, led to the placing of Mission San Francisco de Asís on the Arroyo's banks a few months later. And this placement in turn led to the gradual substitution of the name Dolores (alluding to the Virgin's Sorrows) for the name of St. Francis as the mission's title in popular usage. Traveling south to the end of this arm of the bay, Anza's party discovered a river flowing into it which Font says "we called Rio de Guadalupe."[12] Guadalupe was, of course, the famous spot near Mexico City where the Virgin made her appearance in 1531 to Juan Diego, an Indian peasant. It had already become a national shrine. Hence the town founded on this river's shores in 1777 was known originally as San José de Guadalupe. But time and the secular spirit have shortened this to San José.

Discussion of the influence of the explorers' diaries on mission-naming has taken us far from the mystery of Monterey Bay. In effect, the first Portolá land expedition created the mystery by failing to recognize the bay on their way north, but solved it by more careful examination on their way back to San Diego. Circumstances were not then favorable for founding a Monterey presidio and mission, however. Supplies were at starvation level and winter was approaching. So Portolá decided to return to San Diego to await the coming of the supply ship *San Antonio.*

Arriving back at San Diego on January 25, 1770, Portolá found that the soldiers and civilians he had left there six months before had been living on the food brought up from Baja California for the proposed Mission San Buenaventura.[13] These inroads into its supplies were long to postpone the founding of that mission. On February 10 Portolá dispatched Captain Rivera to the established missions down the peninsula to get the cattle left at San Fernando de Velicatá and everything else edible that he could lay hands on. To Rivera also went the commission to carry "letters and diaries to his Excellency the Viceroy and to the illustrious visitor-general" recounting the events of the expedition just completed. These "diaries" must surely have included, then or later, Crespi's, the most detailed and informative of the lot. Study of these documents by officials and by later explorers did much to fix place names, particularly saints' names, up and down the California coast, and to provide a mine of suggestions for the titles of missions, as noted before.

So precarious and so thinly stretched was the life-line between Alta California and Mexico by sea that nobody at San Diego, from highest to lowest, knew when to expect the packet *San Antonio* bearing desperately needed supplies. Sailing time from the port of San Blas to San Diego averaged nearly two months, and could take longer if the weather was really contrary. Strong head winds blew constantly from the north and west. Nor, of course, could anybody at San Diego know when, or even whether, such a ship had actually left San Blas. This sort of ignorance continued to plague the California missions, presidios, and pueblos alike for years to come, despite the best efforts of an able viceroy like Bucareli to organize the ship sailings on a regular schedule. Only after Alta California became virtually self-supporting did the precise dates of ship departures and arrivals diminish in importance.

Appearance of the *San Antonio* at San Diego on March 19, 1770, (St. Joseph's feast-day) gave Portolá not only welcome new supplies but also a means of transporting to Monterey by sea those members of his company least able to make the laborious march by land. Prominent among these was the lame Fr. Serra, president of the California missions. Accordingly, Portolá divided his party into two groups, one for the land, one for the sea. On April 16 the *San Antonio* sailed for Monterey, and on the next day Portolá led out the land column for the same destination. The *San Antonio* dropped anchor in Monterey Bay on May 31, 1770, watched by the land column, which had reached there several days earlier. June 3 being the feast of the Holy Ghost that day was appointed for the ceremonies of taking possession in the name of Spain.[14]

The military rites of the day pertaining to the founding of a presidio belonged to Commander Portolá. Fr. Serra,

San Carlos Borromeo (Carmel) Mission (founded 1770), in 1903 (top), and in 1975 (bottom).

21

on the other hand, had charge of the religious rituals leading to the founding of the presidio church, and also of the
mission. Obeying the orders of Gálvez, Fr. Serra dedicated
the presidio church to "the most holy patriarch Saint Joseph"
(San José), patron of the whole California enterprise and of
Gálvez himself. But, also in obedience to orders, he entrusted
the mission itself not to Saint Joseph but to San Carlos
Borromeo. Clearly the choice of this saint was dictated by
the fact that both the king of Spain (Carlos III) and the
incumbent viceroy (Carlos de Croix) bore the same first
name. St. Charles Borromeo (1538-1584), archbishop of Mi-
lan, and a cardinal, was a member of the Third Order Secular of St. Francis. He had taken a leading part in the Council
of Trent. But his chief appositeness for a wilderness mission
lay in his care to educate the people of his diocese and to
give them medical aid in plague time. He also insisted that
his lax clergy reform their disordered lives.

Notes

1. Geiger, *Serra,* I, 233.

2. Donald Attwater, *Penguin Dictionary of Saints* (Penguin Books, 1965), and Alban Butler, *Lives of the Saints* 4 vols, ed. and rev. by Herbert Thurston, S.J., and Donald Attwater (New York: J. P. Kenedy, 1956) are my sources for the biographies of all the saints chosen as patrons of the Alta California missions.

3. Fr. Crespi's journal is translated and edited by Herbert E. Bolton, *Historical Memoirs of New California* 4 vols. (New York: Russell & Russell, 1966), II, 113-260.

4. In his September 4, 1769, diary entry, Fr. Crespi named the Hungarian king San Ladislao (1040-95) as patron of the village of Chief Buchon just north of Pismo Beach. It is now called Price Canyon. And on September 7 he called the present Los Osos Valley "La Natividad de Nuestra Señora" (The Nativity of Our Lady). Nobody now seems to remember that either place once bore a holy name. But the bears (*osos*), which the soldiers hunted, live on in name.

5. Ray Brandes, *The Costansó Narrative of the Portolá Expedition* (Hogarth, 1970).

6. Pedro Fages, *A Historical Political and Natural Description of California* tr. Herbert I. Priestly, (Berkeley: Univ. of Calif. Press, 1937), e.g., pp. 15-17.

7. Fages, p. 20.

8. Fr. Pedro Font's diary of the second Anza expedition (1775-76) appears in Bolton IV, 186-469.

9. Bolton IV, 310.

10. Bolton IV, 338.

11. Bolton IV, 346.

12. Bolton IV, 350.

13. Bolton II, 261 ff.

14. Bolton II, 289 ff.

3/Under Governor Fages (1770-74)

As soon as Viceroy de Croix received dispatches in Mexico City reporting the foundations at Monterey, he issued on August 16, 1770, a proclamation publishing the news, amid general rejoicing. At about the same time he received from Fr. Serra a letter containing a request for permission to found additional missions. After a conference with Gálvez the viceroy wrote back to Fr. Serra approving the founding of exactly ten new missions, five of them between San Diego and the port of San Francisco, the other five between San Diego and San Fernando de Vellicatá to extend the mission chain in that area of Baja California connecting the peninsula with Alta California.[1]

As was his right, Viceroy de Croix supplied the names of patron saints for all ten of the projected missions but without assigning any of the ten names to any specific mission. The five south of San Diego were to be under the patronage of San Joaquin (Joachim, father of the Blessed Virgin Mary), Santa Ana (Ann, her mother), San Juan Capistrano (Franciscan missionary, of whom more later on), San Pasqual Baylon (Franciscan lay brother), and San Feliz de Cantalicio (Capuchin lay brother). These five missions in Baja California never actually bore these titles. The Dominicans who replaced the Franciscans in that region in 1773 preferred to substitute specifically Dominican saints' names. Indeed, after Anza opened an overland route to Alta California in 1774 these missions largely lost their intended function as a supply line for goods moving overland to the missions to the north.

Not so the five new missions authorized for Alta California. All those designated by the viceroy were eventually built, though not in the south-to-north sequence he seems to have envisaged for them. His directives read that San Gabriel and Santa Clara missions should be placed in the stretch between San Diego "and the site chosen for that of San Buenaventura." Two others, to be named after San Luis Obispo de Tolosa and San Antonio de Padua, should go between San Buenaventura and San Carlos Boromeo de Monterey. A fifth honoring "our father San Francisco in his own port" was to complete the list.[2] That any specific location had been chosen at this early date for Mission San Buenaventura is more than doubtful. But a situation at about the half-way mark between Mission San Diego and Mission San Carlos Borromeo, possibly on the Santa Barbara Channel, seems to have been in the viceroy's mind. Very likely none of the five new sites had yet been determined. All the viceroy was doing was to suggest a general schema, leaving the pinpointing of sites to the missionaries and the provincial governor, who were familiar with the ground.

Knowing that these ten new missions would require a staff of two missionaries each, Viceroy de Croix ordered the Franciscan College of San Fernando in Mexico City to prepare a reinforcement of thirty missionaries, of whom twenty were to serve in the old missions of Baja California, and ten to man the five new missions planned for the upper part of the territory.[3] In assigning two friars to each of the latter missions Gálvez was accepting another feature of the Franciscan mission system, which called for such numerous and complex activities at a virtually self-sustaining establishment that no one priest could possibly handle them all by himself. This feature of double-staffing every mission was ada- mantly insisted upon by both Fr. Serra and Fr. Lasuén, much to the surprise of the successive governors of the prov- ince, who were accustomed to see missions run by the Je- suits and other Orders with only one priest. The difference was that in such missions the Indians lived not at the mission but in their native rancherías for miles around, where they were administred to from time to time by a peripatetic priest. One priest could manage this, though the resulting conver- sion and education of the surrounding Indians were far less thorough and broadly based than at a Franciscan mission where they lived in daily contact with the priests right on the mission grounds. Herein lay another point of misunder- standing and friction between the missionaries and the gover- nors.

The ten priests dispatched by the College to Alta California sailed from San Blas on the *San Antonio* on January 20, 1771, touched at San Diego on March 12, and went ashore at Monterey on May 21, where Fr. Serra awaited them. The latter now faced a problem in priorities. Which of the five missions he had been charged to found (six if San Buenaven- tura be counted) should be founded first, and what was the best sequence for the remainder? Fr. Serra seems to have begun by doubting that Mission Santa Clara belonged down south in the valley to which Fr. Crespi had given this saint's name on August 9, 1769, and in which the viceroy ap- parently now expected this mission to be situated. It seemed to Fr. Serra to belong, rather, somewhere close to Mission San Francisco de Asís, in recognition of the historical fact that St. Francis had helped St. Clare to establish her sisterhood of Poor Clares at Assisi as a feminine counter- part to his own Order. In other words, Fr. Serra thought it fitting that both these missions should be in the San Fran- cisco Bay area. But he had neither official permission to put

Mission Santa Clara there nor the wherewithal on hand to site two new missions over a hundred miles north of Monterey. So he by-passed the Santa Clara problem temporarily. Better to concentrate first on forging the mission chain between San Diego and Monterey with the four other missions specified by the viceroy.

Accordingly Fr. Serra chose four missionaries for the southermost two of these four missions, San Gabriel and San Buenaventura, and put them aboard the *San Antonio* when it sailed from Monterey for San Diego on June 7, 1771.[4] Four others friars whom he had reserved for the two more northerly missions, San Antonio de Padua and San Luis Obispo de Tolosa, he kept in Monterey, intending to preside himself at the foundation of these missions. The remaining two friars replaced Frs. Gómez and Parrón, who were returning to Mexico on account of ill health.

On June 9, 1771, only two days after the ship sailed, Fr. Serra set out to found Mission San Antonio de Padua, with Frs. Pieras and Sitjar, three sailors, some Indian converts, a mission guard of seven soldiers and a pack train of food, crude farming equipment, building tools and other essentials for starting a Franciscan mission. Fr. Serra, with his usual religious enthusiasm, wanted to site the mission on the spot where Fr. Crespi had said Mass on the anniversary of the day when St. Francis "received the impression of the stigmata on Mount Alberene." To Fr. Serra as a Franciscan that experience, and that spot, had profound mystical meaning. The only trouble with founding a mission there was that nobody, then or now, could be sure exactly where that particular place in the mountains was. Consequently, after taking his party some 25 leagues southward, Fr. Serra eventually chose a location probably considerably north of the one he was seeking.[5]

Still it had most of the qualities needed for a mission site,

San Antonio de Padua Mission (founded 1771), in 1903 (top), and in 1975 (bottom).

except a large Indian population. It also had some water troubles, but these were alleviated later by moving the mission upstream. For the rest it turned out very well. Fr. Serra officially founded Mission San Antonio de Padua on July 14, 1771, the feast day of the great Franciscan, San Buenaventura.[6] San Antonio's day (June 13) had already passed during the preliminary search. As usual at a founding, the priests blessed earth and water, erected a cross, and sang Mass at an altar in a brushwood shelter. San Antonio de Padua (1195-1231) was a Portuguese Franciscan who longed to convert the Moslems of Morocco but was forced back by serious illness to Italy, where he became so learned and powerful a preacher as to be called "hammer of heretics." His private life was notable for its devoutness.

Fr. Serra would have liked nothing better than to go on south immediately to set up the next mission, to be placed under the patronage of San Luis Obispo de Tolosa in the Los Osos region. But no soldiers were available to guard it, and supplies of all sorts were very low. So he returned instead to Monterey to supervise the removal of Mission San Carlos five miles southwestward to the Carmel River valley.

Probably Fr. Serra never intended to allow the mission to remain in the presidio where it had been first situated. Although the original foundation had been made on June 3, 1770, the viceroy was already giving his consent to the removal in a letter of November 12, 1770.[7] Not only were water and agricultural land more plentiful at Carmel, but also the Franciscans were already experiencing the expected disadvantages of the presidio location. At Monterey few Indians dared come in for conversions, and those who did come were subjected to manifold temptations and corruptions by the soldiers. The transfer of Mission San Carlos to Carmel was completed by December 1771, under Fr. Serra's direction. It could now start to prosper under a semi-independent life of its own. In September, 1773, Fr. Palóu, for the same reasons, moved Mission San Diego about six miles, upriver and eastward, from the presidio on the harbor there.

But to go back to the summer of 1771. In the days before the *San Antonio* sailed for San Diego on June 7 with the four missionaries instructed to found Missions San Buenaventura and San Gabriel, Fr. Serra discussed with Commander Fages the best sites for those two missions. Fages had traversed the country between San Diego and Monterey on foot three times, on the two Portolá land expeditions, whereas Fr. Serra had only sailed along the coast from San Diego to Monterey. Fages' observations of the terrain, probably combined with a study of Fr. Crespi's diaries, led the two men to the decision "that the mission of San Gabriel should be founded with ten soldiers on the river named Jesus de los Temblores, known by the soldiers as the Santa Ana River, and that of San Buenaventura in the first town of the Channel of Santa Barbara, named Asumpta, with a guard of fifteen men in view of the large numbers of heathen seen on the channel."[8] Fages then sailed on the *San Antonio* to San Diego with the missionaries in order to guide them to these selected sites and to provide their military guard from the San Diego garrison.

The *San Antonio* dropped anchor at San Diego on July 14. Frs. Angel Somera and Benito Cambón, appointed by Fr. Serra to found Mission San Gabriel, set forth on August 6 with ten soldiers and a pack train of supplies. When they arrived at the Río de Jesús de Temblores, however, they found the area quite unsuitable for a mission. The frequency of earthquakes there no doubt affected this decision. So they went on six leagues farther "to the valley of San Miguel, and near the river of this name, not far from its source" they found a location where plentiful water flowed through fertile land. There they set to work on the founding and performed the necessary official ceremonies on "the 8th of September, 1771, the day of the nativity of Our Lady." That a mission under the patronage of Gabriel, the Archangel of the Annunciation to Mary, should be dedicated on her birthday was of course most apt.[9]

The new foundation, however, began under a cloud of troubles. So many Indians of doubtful disposition soon came crowding round to watch the building of a church, living quarters, and the customary stockade, that on October 1 Fr. Somera returned to San Diego with the empty pack train to ask Commander Fages for more soldiers. He was back in San Gabriel on October 9 with the only two men that Commander Fages felt he could spare. On the very next day a crowd of Indians attacked the mission guard with arrows, contending that a soldier had assaulted an Indian woman. In the fray that followed, an Indian chief was killed by the soldiers and his head hung on the stockade. But the two priests managed to patch up a peace.

At that point Fages himself arrived with the party he was guiding to Asumpta to found Mission San Buenaventura, as agreed with Fr. Serra. On hearing of the tense situation at Mission San Gabriel, he judged it essential to reinforce the garrison there with some of the troops destined for the proposed Mission San Buenaventura. That left him, he considered, with too weak a force to protect the latter. So he resolved to postpone the San Buenaventura founding, and departed with the remainder of his men for the capital at Monterey, where he thought they would be needed if the Indians in the north should become rebellious. The two priests intended for San Buenaventura he left at San Gabriel. San Buenaventura was not to get his mission for another eleven years.[10]

During the winter of 1771-1772 the tribes around Monterey showed no signs of unrest. Apparently both Commander

San Gabriel Arcangel Mission (founded 1771), in 1903 (top), and in 1975 (bottom).

33

Fages and Fr. Serra then bethought themselves of the viceroy's command of late 1770 to found a mission in honor of "our Father San Francisco in his own port."[11] Consequently in March 1772, Fages left Monterey with a small squad of soldiers to explore the Berkeley side of the Bay, still under the misapprehension that the whole Bay was merely one large water obstacle to be got around if he, or anyone else, was to reach the true San Francisco Bay (now Drake's Bay) farther north along the coast. Fr. Serra sent along Fr. Crespi to keep one of his painstaking diaries, with special attention to nothing good mission sites. Baffled by the immense stretches of water which he could not cross, Fages headed back to Monterey. The terrain traversed by the expedition did not appeal to Fr. Crespi as good for missions, either, and he gave Fr. Serra a discouraging report on that score.

In sum, the Berkeley side yielded no positive results. Disappointed, Fr. Serra turned his eyes southward. He would have liked to begin extending the "mission ladder," as he called it, south from Mission San Antonio. But the yearly supply ships from Mexico had failed to appear that spring, and everybody in the already established missions was hungry, not to mention the presidios. This was not the time for increasing their number. Even down San Diego way the need was acute. Gathering what food could be spared from their reserves, Capt. Fages and Fr. Serra sent it by mule train to Missions San Gabriel and San Diego. Then Fages took a squad of his men to hunt bears in Los Osos Valley, where they had been observed to abound. There the hunters spent three summer months, and were able to send a number of mule-loads of dried bear meat to help feed the Monterey presidio and the two northern missions. The day was yet to come when vast herds of cattle, sheep, goats and swine, and abundant grain crops would enable the missions to feed the whole territory when necessary.

At last in early August, 1772, news reached Monterey of the arrival of the *San Carlos* and the *San Antonio* at San Diego with the long-awaited supplies. But another obstacle had arisen. The ship captains were refusing to set sail for Monterey through stormy seas. Fr. Scrra determined to go forthwith overland to San Diego to change their minds, and on the way down "to found in passing, the mission of San Luis Obispo de Tolosa in the Valley of Los Osos, which was the place designated for that mission."[12] Who so designated the place, and when, is not known, but the likelihood is that Fages persuaded Fr. Serra of its attractions when he resolved to accompany Fr. Serra's party to San Diego. This party included Fr. José Cavaller, chosen by Fr. Serra more than a year before to take charge of Mission San Luis Obispo when it should be formed, but not his intended colleague and friend, Fr. Juncosa, who acted temporarily as Fr. Serra's substitute in Monterey.

Versions of the date when Fr. Serra's party reached Los Osos differ. Some say August 19; others, August 29. The latter is certainly right if the party left Monterey as late as August 24, as Fr. Geiger reports. Moreover, August 19 is the feast-day of San Luis Obispo, and if Fr. Serra had arrived on that day he would surely have made every effort to found the mission at once. Instead, he founded it on September 1, 1772, presumably after looking over the region for the best possible location.[13] He chose well, a site on a fertile plain drained by several streams. Unlike many other missions, Mission San Luis Obispo never has had to be moved.

Its patron, St. Louis (1274-1297), Bishop of Toulouse, France, had been heir to the throne of Naples and Sicily. After being trained in boyhood by the Franciscans at Barcelona, he chose to give up his throne so that he might join their Order. At the age of twenty-three he was ordained Bishop of Toulouse. He was to live less than a year afterwards, but during his brief tenure he excelled in the pastoral care of his diocese. Buried first in the Franciscan church at Marseilles, his body was later reinterred at Valencia, where many miracles occurred at his grave. Thereafter he was revered as a major Franciscan saint. As a sign of this reverence, Fr. Crespi, on August 21, 1769, during the first Portolá expedition, had put two Indian villages under his protection farther south.

Fr. Serra left with Fr. Cavaller at the new mission five soldiers and two Baja California Indian converts. But he had few worldly goods of any kind to give them. For food he let them have, out of his own scanty store, a few handfuls of seed grains, fifty pounds of flour, a little chocolate and a box of sugar to trade with the Chumash Indians of the valley for seeds. With these, several lame mules and a few tools. Commending the eight men to the care of God, Fr. Serra hastened on south on September 2. As he passed through the populous villages along the Santa Barbara Channel he made up his mind that at least three missions ought to be planted there. Since Fr. Crespi's diary had called attention to the large rancheria of Asumpta as ideal for a mission, Fr. Serra and Capt. Fages explored the territory surrounding it, and agreed that Mission San Buenaventura, when established, would do well there.[14]

Reaching San Diego on September 16 the two leaders lost no time in straightening out the hesitations and confusions involving the two supply ships in the harbor. Fr. Serra persuaded Captain Pérez of the *San Antonio* to sail his vessel to Monterey. Also, on September 27 Frs. Crespi and Dumetz took a pack-train north with food for the hungry missions along the way. The second ship the *San Carlos,* being now unloaded, prepared to return to San Blas. But it re-

San Luís Obispo Mission (founded 1772), in 1903 (top), and in 1975 (bottom).

ceived an unexpected passenger, Fr. Serra himself. The constant conflicts between friars and soldiers at the missions over the question as to who had what authority there, particularly in controlling and disciplining the resident Indians, had opened up the basic problem as to who should be running the missions. Capt. Fages championed his soldiers, while Fr. Presidente Serra of course supported his missionaries. A good deal of personal irritation between the two men naturally resulted. It came to a head in San Diego so alarmingly that Fr. Serra, after consultation with the friars there, resolved to lay the case before the viceroy himself. On October 20, 1772, he sailed from San Diego aboard the *San Carlos,* landed at San Blas on November 4, and entered Mexico City on February 6, 1773.[15]

In the interviews which followed, Fr. Serra found in Viceroy Bucareli a sympathetic, devout, yet brilliantly practical man whose friendship over a period of eight years could be depended upon to aid the Alta California missions at a critical time in their growth. At Bucareli's suggestion Fr. Serra submitted to him on March 13 a written *Representación* of 32 points affecting the relations between all the elements involved in mission problems—from Indians, missionaries, soldiers and sailors, governors, colonists and postal officials to institutions like the Franciscan colleges and the civil administration in Mexico City.[16]

The meeting of his viceregal council which Bucareli convoked on May 6, 1773, decided for Fr. Serra on almost every point.[17] Giving him exactly what he wanted, the council decreed that "the government, control, and education of the baptized Indians should belong exclusively to the missionaries." The latter were to have over the Indians the extensive powers which Spanish law allowed to parents over their children in education, in economic affairs, and in punishing all crimes except murder. Moreover, as Fr. Serra had requested, Bucareli removed Capt. Fages from his office as governor, but without staining his record with a reprimand. In his place an experienced soldier, Capt. Fernando Rivera y Moncada, who had taken part in the Portolá expeditions, became governor, though Fr. Serra would have preferred Lt. Ortega.

Notes

1. Bolton, *Historical Memoirs* II, 308; Engelhardt, *Missions and Missionaries* II, 82.

2. Bolton II, 311.

3. Bolton II, 308; Engelhardt II, 82-5.

4. Bolton II, 313-14; Engelhardt II, 85 ff.

5. Bolton II, 315 ff.

6. Bolton II, 316.

7. Geiger, *Serra* I, 274.

8. Bolton II, 321.

9. Bolton II, 324 ff.: The ceremonies were those commonly used in founding a mission: ". . . raising the holy cross, standard of our redemption, in a small shelter of branches which served temporarily for a church, they celebrated the first Mass . . . They immediately set to work to build a church of logs and tule, and some humble dwellings for the fathers and the soldiers."

10. Bolton II, 327.

11. Bolton II, 328-55, gives Fr. Crespi's journal of this 1772 Fages expedition to San Francisco.

12. Bolton II, 358.

13. Bolton II, 361; Geiger I, 324 ff.

14. Bolton II, 365. In his diary entry for August 14, 1769, Crespi had called the town "La Asunción de Nuestra Señora" (The Assumption of Our Lady). The name soon was shortened to "Asumpta." See Bolton II, 147.

15. Geiger I, 337-50, 357.

16. Geiger I, 371-80.

17. Geiger I, 381-87.

4/Under Governor Rivera (1774-77)
San Francisco Bay

His aims accomplished, Fr. Serra left Mexico City in mid-September, 1773, sailed from San Blas on January 25, 1774, aboard the new frigate *Santiago,* and disembarked at San Diego on March 14. His journey of six months for the one-way trip from Mexico City took somewhat more time than usual, but it illustrates the sorts of delays which made communications between the capital and Alta California so slow. Fr. Serra had been away from his California missions for about seventeen months, during which Fr. Palóu, his substitute, had thought it best not to try to set up any new missions in Fr. Serra's absence, but he had moved Mission San Diego some six miles inland away from the presidio, a step to which Fr. Serra gave his hearty approval. Serra then decided to take a leisurely trip of inspection northward from mission to mission. Before he was ready to leave San Diego he was amazed to learn on March 25 that Anza had arrived a few days before at Mission San Gabriel, thereby opening up for the first time an overland route from Sonora to Alta California. While in Mexico City Fr. Serra had strongly advocated such a journey by Anza but had not expected him to arrive so soon. Anza's new route provided a welcome alternative to ocean shipping, but it depended on two chief variables, the large numbers of mules required and the friendliness of the Yuma Indians along the way.

Fr. Serra stopped over at Mission San Gabriel from April 12 to 23, but Anza had long since left for Monterey. The two leaders finally met on April 28 somewhere near Point Concepción and spent an evening talking together. By then Anza, having seen Monterey, was making his usual dazzling speed back to Mexico to report to Bucareli on his accomplishments. Fr. Serra after the meeting with Anza continued his quiet progress northward, entering Monterey on May 11, followed on May 23, 1774, by Capt. Rivera, who took over the office of governor from Fages.

The stage was thus set for the next round of disagreements over the founding of the missions and related problems, the new governor holding back cautiously, Fr. Serra all in favor of pushing ahead. Fr. Serra had discovered in his recent itinerary among the missions the welcome fact that they had, if anything, a surplus of priests who could be used to staff new establishments. San Diego had three, San Gabriel four, San Luis Obispo three, San Antonio three, and San Carlos three besides himself. On June 21, 1774, he wrote a letter to Bucareli calling his attention to the surplus of priests for the five missions and expressing hope that Governor Rivera would press on with the important business of founding some of the other missions long projected.

Fr. Serra might have for the moment an oversupply of priests, but Rivera did not feel that he had any oversupply of soldiers, considering that the whole of Alta California lay under the protection of only a few dozen troops, many of them scattered in small groups of five or six as guards among the missions over hundreds of miles. As an experienced military man Rivera would have preferred to have these scanty forces united in presidios where they would be under military discipline and quickly available in case of attack by foreign ships from the sea or by the many thousands of unsubjugated Indians by land. He had nothing against missionaries. No doubt if he could have had a strong presidio near each mission he would have been delighted to help set up a hundred missions. But from Rivera's point of view his lines were already dangerously overextended. And the more new missions arose, with demands for more of his troops as guards, the more overextended these lines would be. This difference between the missionary drive to convert the pagans in all districts and the military need to maintain large centralized fighting units for the protection of the province underlay many of the irritations and misunderstandings between Fr. Serra and successive governors.

One incident to illustrate this difference arose almost immediately. On or before July 18, 1774, Fr. Serra urged Rivera to found the long-awaited Mission San Buenaventura.[1] Rivera refused on the ground that he could not spare any soldiers for guards. Serra then proposed that if six could be detached from the Monterey presidio he would contribute three from the guards of Mission San Carlos. With these nine Mission San Buenaventura would surely be safe. Not wanting to weaken either the presidio or the guard at Mission San Carlos, Rivera returned so categorical a refusal that Fr. Serra concluded, perhaps unjustly, that Rivera would go on saying No even if scores of additional soldiers could be added by some miracle to the Alta California presidios.

At the same conference other issues between soldiers and friars came to the surface. Fr. Serra asked Rivera to remove a corporal at Mission San Luis Obispo who was giving a bad example to converts by his sexual immorality. Rivera refused; he was not going to shift his soldiers around to please a missionary who might become dissatisfied with one of them. For the same reason he would not move immoral majordomos from one mission to another, or recall them to Monterey. Also, Fr. Serra complained that Rivera was keeping at the presidio and slaughtering for his soldiers the cattle earmarked for the future Missions San Francisco and Santa Clara. The animals should be delivered to Carmel for safekeeping. Rivera pointed out that his men were hungry, and where else were they to get food? And if Fr. Serra regretted that the rations for the workmen at the missions had just been cut in half by Rivera, they had been eating full government rations long enough. Let the missions provide. On July 18 Fr. Serra wrote a detailed report of the meeting with Rivera to his superiors in the College of San Fernando.

On August 6, 1774, Fr. Palóu received from Bucareli a letter dated May 25, stating the viceroy's wish that Mission San Francisco be founded as soon as exploration of the Bay uncovered a fitting location. This letter Fr. Palóu of course gave to Fr. Serra, who in turn showed it to Rivera, only to draw the latter's inevitable shrug of dismissal, with the remark that he had as yet neither the soldiers nor the necessary munitions.[2] But as the autumn went on, the families and the soldiers whom Rivera had gathered in Sinaloa before coming to Monterey arrived at the presidio there. The governor now had soldiers to spare.

On November 20, 1774, therefore, Rivera took sixteen soldiers and Fr. Palóu to survey the San Francisco Bay area in preparation for the founding of missions.[3] They went up the peninsula on the Bay's west side, noting possible mission sites. On December 4 Fr. Palóu planted a cross on its northern tip. Fatefully, the expedition returned to Monterey, not by the inland route but along the sea-coast as Portolá's had done in 1769. Fr. Palóu adopted all the place-names Fr. Crespi had bestowed along that route. In particular he echoed Fr. Crespi's praise of the site on the San Lorenzo River where Mssion Santa Cruz would one day stand. And Fr. Palóu added that it was "fit not only for a town, but even for a city, for nothing necessary is lacking to it." By this enthusiasm he may have helped to draw to Santa Cruz in 1797 the attention of the founders of Villa Branciforte, with disastrous results to the mission. But that is a later story.

Rivera's expedition was back in Monterey on December 13. Fr. Palóu handed his diary to Fr. Serra, who forwarded a copy of it to Bucareli on January 8, 1775. The diary reported favorably on potential mission sites in the general area of the Bay. Fr. Serra's accompanying letter reminded the viceroy that, whatever was done at San Francisco, four more missions still should be founded between San Diego and Monterey in order to convert all the tribes along that populous stretch of country, of which two missions should be for the Chumash Indians on the Santa Barbara Channel: San Buenaventura and Santa Clara. Because only one mission had been authorized so far for San Francisco Bay Fr. Serra was still thinking of Mission Santa Clara as officially assigned to the south, where Fr. Crespi's diary had recommended that it be placed.

The situation changed radically, however, with Bucareli's next letter arriving at Monterey on the *San Carlos* on June 18, 1775. It ordered the establishment of not one but two missions, and also a presidio, in the San Francisco Bay region. In aid of that purpose, the viceroy wrote, Anza was organizing a second overland expedition, much larger than the first, which would bring to Monterey soldiers, settlers, and supplies for these new establishments. Fr. Serra now had assurance of two more missions in the north, but he kept on urging the need for others in the south.[4] Bucareli answered this plea by sending a letter which Rivera received on August 9, 1775, ordering that a mission be set up between Missions San Diego and San Gabriel.

Further explorations of San Francisco Bay in the summer of 1775 gave a new dimension of importance to Anza's second land expedition. Capt. Ayala's painstaking survey by ship of the interior of the Bay settled once and for all that it was quite separate from the open roadstead which we now call Drake's Bay but which the Spaniards had been calling San Francisco for many years. This information likewise revealed the strategic location of the peninsula as controlling the only sea entrance to the Bay through the Golden Gate, and hence as furnishing an ideal location for a presidio and missions from a military point of view. So Anza's second expedition left Mexico in September, 1775, under explicit instructions: " . . . with the object of bringing troops and families to occupy the port of our Seraphic Father San Francisco, with the intention of founding there a fort or presidio, and two missions in the neighborhood, assigning to each one of them six soldiers, and eighteen to the presidio or fort, besides some families of settlers."[5]

This insistence by Bucareli on the soldiers' being married and taking their families to California with them, and on civilian settlers doing the same, shows his intention not solely to build military strength on the Bay but also to create the beginnings of a civilian population. Anza was able to offer his recruits government subsidies and help in getting settled. Nevertheless finding men and families willing, in effect, to emigrate from Mexico took him months of patient search in Mexico City, Sinaloa, and Sonora. At last he managed to assemble thirty married soldiers with their families, and twelve families of civilian settlers, a total of two hundred thirty souls. They brought with them all their wordly possessions which could be loaded on mules, horses, and cattle. Their trek was a forerunner in miniature of the Westward Movement across the Great Plains in the next century. But they had nothing like the Conestoga wagons, and accordingly were much more limited in what they could transport. As chaplain and diarist they had Fr. Pedro Font, a Franciscan from the College of Santa Cruz de Querétaro, whose orientation seems to have been more Mexican than Spanish.

Well before Anza left Mexico Bucareli wrote to both Fr. Serra and Governor Rivera to prepare them for his coming. Letters to that effect reached Monterey on August 10, 1775,[6] and Anza's long column did not appear at Mission San Gabriel until January 4, 1776. The letter to Fr. Serra merely repeated the instructions to Anza and required Fr. Serra to be ready to establish "two missions and a fort . . . in the vicinity of the harbor of San Francisco" as soon as Anza got to Monterey. But the letter to Rivera added an instruction that he co-operate with Fr. Serra in founding, besides the two San Francisco missions, "one or two more missions in places that might be judged most suitable, assigning some of the soldiers from the presidios, in the meantime adding to them some from the nearest missions."

Soon after receipt of these letters Fr. Serra and Gov. Rivera met to consider what was required of them. Their instructions called for the founding of not only two missions and a fort in and about the San Francisco region but also "one or two" more with unspecified names at unspecified places. Since the San Francisco foundations must await the coming of Anza's column, the two men agreed that they had better get the others founded before it arrived, if possible. They agreed also that one of them should be "between San Diego and San Gabriel, in the place named San Juan Capistrano (in Fr. Crespi's 1769 diary), or in any other place in that neighborhood where greater advantages might be found." Nearness to the supply port of San Diego seems to have been the governing factor in this choice. In speeding up the time element Rivera was probably not sorry to put himself one-up on the highly favored Anza.[7]

Fr. Serra did not himself go south for the founding of mission San Juan Capistrano but entrusted it to the experienced hands of Fr. Lasuén of Monterey and Fr. Amurrió of San Luis Obispo. Before the end of August, 1775, these two friars set out, Fr. Amurrió to collect at Mission San Gabriel livestock for the projected mission, Fr. Lasuen to confer with Sgt. Ortega at San Diego presidio and to examine, with his aid, not only Fr. Crespi's San Juan Capistrano valley but other sites between San Diego and San Gabriel which might be even more advantageous. By October 30 Fr. Lasuén had fixed on what he considered the best location, not in Fr. Crespi's valley but some miles north of it.[8] This location offered excellent water, soil, and trees for timber, besides being near El Camino Real at a point some twenty leagues from San Gabriel and slightly more from San Diego. Here, then, Mission San Juan Capistrano was to rise.

Why was the new mission given San Juan Capistrano as its patron? The viceroy in 1770 had included his name among those to be assigned to the five missions contemplated south of San Diego in Baja California, but not among the five planned for the north. No doubt Fr. Crespi's bestowal of the name in 1769 on a valley near San Diego had its effect too, and the mention of it in the conference between Fr. Serra and Gov. Rivera even more. The final selection of this saint as patron may well have been made by Fr. Lasuén himself on the spot.

On October 30, 1775, the last day of the octave of San Juan Capistrano, Fr. Lasuén began the construction of a chapel and living quarters for the priests with the help of friendly Indians. But he did not perform any ceremonies founding the mission. He seems to have been waiting for Fr. Amurrió. The latter arrived with the livestock from Mission San Gabriel on November 8. But on that same day, before the founding ceremonies could be started, a messenger from San Diego rode up post-haste with news of a serious Indian attack on the mission there.[9] The commander of the soldiers guarding construction work at the new mission site immediately departed for San Diego with all his men. The two missionaries then decided that they could not remain without protection. So they too left the work unfinished, stopping only to bury two heavy mission bells in order to hide them. With everything portable, and with the livestock, they rode back to San Diego. Governor Rivera also hurried there all the way from Monterey to take charge of the situation.

So the groundwork was laid for the future Mission San Juan Capistrano, and so it was abandoned with the mission still unfounded. Its patron (1386-1456), a bold spirit, might not have approved of so precipitate a retreat. A Franciscan mission preacher throughout Italy for many years, he had also dealt severely with the Hussite heretics in Austria, preached a crusade against the Turks, accompanied Hunyadi in his military campaigns against them, and died of plague in the course of one such campaign. Work on his mission in California was not to be continued and dedicated until a year later.

Governor Rivera lingered on at the San Diego presidio for many months into 1776, but was too alarmed by the spectre of a general Indian uprising to give any thought to the unfinished mission. Hearing of this long delay, and concerned equally about Mission San Diego, which had been abandoned after the Indian attack, Fr. Serra sailed from Monterey on the *San Antonio*, which dropped anchor in San Diego harbor on July 11, 1776. Armed with letters of authority from Viceroy Bucareli he first rebuilt the burned out Mission San Diego in its same location several miles inland from the presidio.[10] Then he led a company of priests and workers back to the gaping walls and buried bells of the San Juan Capistrano site, "saying the first Mass in it on the first day of November, the great feast of All Saints, in the year 1776." On that day the Mission officially came into existence. In the three and a half months since his arrival Fr. Serra's energy had restored two missions to usefulness.

Months before, Fr. Serra's long dream of a mission at San Francisco Bay dedicated to the great founder of his Order had been realized, though without his presence there. It began to happen when Anza's second expedition reached Monterey by land from Mexico on March 10, 1776, with its long train of married soldiers and settlers bringing all their worldly goods for starting a new life.[11] On March 22 Anza set off with Fr. Font and a compact band of ten soldiers under Lt. Moraga for a quick survey of the peninsula on the west side of the Bay, which he had never seen before.[12] Having agreed previously with Governor Rivera not to found any missions there until Rivera returned from San Diego, Anza left the rest of his people safely but uncomfortably perched at Monterey.

Anza had never promised, however, not to scout for eligible sites. In the course of doing so he picked a presidio site which soon became accepted as the official one. The names he gave to a nearby arroyo (Nuestra Señora de Dolores: Our Lady of Sorrows) and to a river at the Bay's south end (Nuestra Señora de Guadalupe, in honor of the Blessed Virgin's appearance at Guadalupe in Mexico in 1531) both stuck, as narrated earlier in the discussion of Fr. Font's diaries. Not yet mentioned are Anza's predictions that both the Arroyo and the Río would make fine locations for missions. These predictions were to be borne out before long, though not by Anza personally.

After taking a brief look at the east side of the Bay,

San Juan Capistrano Mission (founded 1776), in 1903 (top), and in 1975 (bottom).

Anza rode back into Monterey on April 8, 1776, with his usual quick efficiency.[13] From there he wrote to Rivera an account of what he had accomplished, and waited some days for a reply. He had not broken his pledge to Rivera not to found missions, but Rivera seems to have thought that Anza had violated the spirit of their accord by searching out potential sites too definitively. At any rate Rivera was affronted and wrote no letter in reply. Instead, he started north from San Diego, where he had multiplied his own troubles by incurring a sentence of excommunication from the priests of the mission for violating the right of sanctuary claimed by an Indian rebel. In that frame of mind it was easy for him to quarrel with Anza. And the latter, having waited in vain for a reply to his letter, was equally ready to reciprocate.

Leaving in Monterey under the command of Lt. Moraga most of the soldiers and all of the civilians he had brought from Mexico, he started on the return journey. He and Rivera met on El Camino Real. The contest of words and insulting silences which ensued was no credit to either man. No reconciliation occurred. Still seething, Anza hastened back to Mexico City. His report to Bucareli in late May, 1776, taken together with the Franciscans' account of their excommunication of Rivera, resulted in Rivera's recall in 1777 and his replacement by Felipe de Neve as governor. After listening to Anza, Bucareli also wrote urgently to Monterey that no further delay in founding the presidio and two missions at San Francisco should be tolerated.[14]

The demotion of Rivera, the second governor to lose his footing in slippery California, has its tragic side. So long as Mexico had a viceroy who backed the California missionaries to the hilt, as Bucareli did, any man who wished to remain governor must win their support by promoting their missions as the heart of the California enterprise, even at the expense of yielding some points in what he might regard as short term military safety. Rivera, however, was a stubborn soldier and no compromiser. His failure to win the confidence of the padres, or the viceroy, or Anza seems to have shaken his nerve and isolated him. The padres were always lamenting the loneliness of their work at the missions. But they had one another, they had a careful shepherd in Fr. Serra, and from Mexico City came the friendly help both of their own college and of the viceroy. By comparison the governor was by far the lonelier. Rivera's vain, pathetic attempts to get Fr. Lasuén, whom he liked, assigned to him as his personal chaplain illustrate his needs. Increasingly frustrated and alone, he rushed into rash decisions or became unable to make any decisions at all.

Before his recall by the viceroy became known to Rivera he wrote early in May, 1776, from San Diego to Lt. Moraga in Monterey to take twenty soldiers and found the San Francisco presidio "on the site designated by . . . De Anza," but to postpone "for the present" the erecting of any missions near the Bay.[15] At the same time Rivera ordered twelve married soldiers and their families left by Anza at Mission San Gabriel as an enlargement of its garrison to proceed to Monterey. All the elements of Anza's expedition thus became reunited there under the command of his second in command, Lt. Moraga, who now had almost embarrassing numbers of soldiers and settlers but explicit orders from Rivera not to create missions in which to plant them.

So on June 17, 1776, Lt. Moraga left Monterey for San Francisco, nominally to construct only a presidio. The composition of his party, however, suggests a wider if unspoken purpose. He took north with him by land not only the twenty soldiers specified by Rivera but also their families, as well as seven civilian families, and herdsmen and muleteers driving two hundred cattle and a well-loaded mule train.[16] Significantly, too, Frs. Cambón and Palóu came along, commissioned by Fr. Serra to examine possible mission sites.

That was only the land party. When the supply ship *San Carlos* sailed into Monterey Bay on June 3, her cargo designated for Monterey was promptly unloaded, but someone mysteriously ordered her to take aboard "provisions which had been stored in the warehouse since the previous year as belonging to San Francisco." Also taken on board were the greater part of the tools for the soldiers and settlers who were to go to the new foundations . . ." as well as "the vestments and utensils for house and field belonging to the first mission that was to be founded in the neighborhood of the harbor of San Francisco upon the arrival of the *San Carlos.*"[17] In other words, supplies for both a presidio and a mission were to be carried by water to a rendezvous with Lt. Moraga's party at San Francisco. Bucareli's command to situate *two* missions in that region apparently had not had time enough to reach Monterey from Mexico City. The expedition still acted officially under Rivera's orders not to found any missions at all. But it is queer how all things conspired together to provide the priests, the soldiers, the religious goods and the farming equipment needed for the forming of a mission.

Fr. Palóu of course kept the journal. He records that on June 27 the entire party camped "on the bank of a lagoon called by Señor Anza Nuestra Señora de los Dolores," intending to await there the coming of the *San Carlos* and meantime to look about for the best presidio location.[18] Frs. Palóu and Cambón, however, had made up their minds that they wanted no better spot for a mission than the one on which they already stood. Accordingly only two days later they built a brushwood chapel, and on June 29, "the feast of the great, holy apostles, San Pedro and San Pablo,"

San Francisco de Asís (Dolores) Mission (founded 1776), in 1903 (top), and in 1975 (bottom).

said the first Mass in it. These actions did not quite constitute the official founding of a mission but they came close to it. [19]

By July 26 the *San Carlos* still had not appeared. Then Lt. Moraga chose a spot "near the white cliff for the presidio site," moved his camp there on that date, and began building tule huts as temporary dwellings for soldiers and their families. The two priests remained at their brushwood chapel on Dolores lagoon. Lt. Moraga tacitly acknowledged its developing status as a mission by sending there the usual guard of six soldiers, and all the properties and livestock marked as belonging to a San Francisco Bay mission. He even ordered these soldiers to cut timbers for the first mission buildings at that location. [20]

When the *San Carlos* eventually came in on August 18, 1776, work on the presidio and the presumed new mission went forward simultaneously. Sailors from the ship gave their help in putting up the mission church and living quarters for the priests. Formal possession of the presidio was taken on September 17, the day of "the impression of the stigmata of our Seraphic Father San Francisco . . . since he is the patron of the harbor, the new presidio, and the mission." And although the mission had been unofficially begun on June 29, formal founding was scheduled to take place on October 4, the feast day of St. Francis. Lt. Moraga's absence until October 9 caused a postponement. On that date it became Mission San Francisco de Asís. [21]

Lt. Moraga considered it a great advantage for all concerned that the mission was not more than a mile or two from the presidio. At that distance it would supply food and a labor force for the presidio, and besides be easy to protect. Through the circumstance that the site of the mission became set before that of the presidio, Frs. Palóu and Cambón found themselves giving tacit approval to the fait accompli of this

proximity. Had Fr. Serra been there with them his unhappy
experiences at both San Diego and Monterey with this kind
of proximity might have caused him to insist on moving the
mission a number of miles down the peninsula. But Fr.
Serra was far away in the south at this time, rebuilding the
burned Mission San Diego and resuming construction of the
abondoned Mission San Juan Capistrano. The latter he
founded officially on November 1, 1776. Perhaps he did not
expect the erection of a San Francisco mission quite so soon,
or perhaps he considered the problems of the south as equally vital. In any case, after finishing his work at Mission San
Juan Capistrano he proceeded slowly northward, mission by
mission, to Monterey, where his next business turned out to
be the founding of Mission Santa Clara, about two days'
journey to the north.

The question of the proper placement of this mission had
a considerable history behind it. As far back as 1770 Viceroy
de Croix had requested a Mission Santa Clara somewhere
between Mission San Diego and Mission San Buenaventura.
Presumably he had in mind a valley which Fr. Crespi's
journal had named Santa Clara under the dates of August
9 to 12, 1769. Fr. Serra went along with this idea of a
southern location until on June 18, 1775, he received from
Viceroy Bucareli a letter authorizing two missions at San
Francisco Bay, as narrated earlier. That naturally changed
his views about the site for Mission Santa Clara. Knowing
the history of his Order, Fr. Serra was too keenly aware
of the close association between St. Francis of Assisi and St.
Clare of the same city during their lives to want the missions
dedicated to them to be widely separated. If Mission San
Francisco de Asís rose near the tip of the peninsula at San
Francisco Bay, Mission Santa Clara should certainly be
paired with it in the same area. In preparation for that event
Fr. Serra appointed Frs. Murguía and Tomás de la Peña as

its missionaries.

By Christmas, 1776, Bucareli was writing to ask Fr. Serra whether Mission Santa Clara had been founded yet. Happily, Governor Rivera had been exploring the peninsula late in November in order to pick a site for such a mission.[22] He had with him Fr. Tomás de la Peña to act as its religious founder. As it happened, before the governor could choose a fitting place he was called away to Mission San Luis Obispo by reports of Indian attacks there. Having pursued and arrested the malefactors, he sent word to Lt. Moraga at the San Francisco Presidio to go ahead with the choice of site and the dedication of Mission Santa Clara. Apparently it was already assumed implicitly or explicitly, that it would be placed somewhere along Anza's Rio de Nuestra Señora de Guadalupe, some forty miles south of Mission San Francisco de Asís.

Consequently, early in January, 1777, Lt. Moraga gathered the soldiers and their families who were to guard the new mission, accompanied by Fr. Tomás de la Peña, who was to found it.[23] Reaching the Rio on January 7, they spent a few days looking for the best land along the stream. They found it, as they thought, by January 12, and on that date Fr. de la Peña raised and blessed the Cross and sang the first Mass to found Alta California's eighth mission. St. Clare of Assisi (1194–1253) was one of the earliest followers of St. Francis and with his aid organized the Poor Clares in 1215 as a sisterhood of nuns vowed to Franciscan principles of religious life.

As it turned out later, the site for Mission Santa Clara had not been very wisely chosen. In 1784 flooding from the river forced its removal to higher ground not far away. Then in 1818 an earthquake leveled the new church erected on that ground, and another move some miles farther on had to be undertaken. These were catastrophes of nature.

Santa Clara de Asís Mission (founded 1777), in 1903 (top), and in 1975 (bottom).

Another sort of blow fell in November, 1777, the very year of the mission's foundation, when a group of Anza colonists came north from Monterey at the urging of Governor Neve to found the pueblo of San José de Guadalupe on the other side of the river, not much more than a stones throw from the mission.   This secular settlement cost the priests all the usual disturbances to their instruction of their neophytes in Christian principles. Disputes even arose between mission and pueblo over the boundaries between their lands. These disputes dragged on for years, and were not adjudicated until 1801. Relations between a mission and a pueblo proved to be hardly less difficult than those between a mission and a presidio.

Notes

1. Geiger, *Serra* I, 433.

2. Geiger I, 443.

3. Bolton, *Historical Memoirs* III, 248–308, translates Fr. Palóu's diary of the expedition.

4. Bolton IV, 57 ff.

5. Bolton IV, 80.

6. Geiger II, 35 ff.

7. Bolton IV, 57–8.

8. Bolton IV, 59.

9. Bolton IV, 59.

10. Geiger II, 114.

11. Bolton IV, 88 ff. A group of about a dozen riders, two of them representing De Anza and Fr. Font, reenacted this expedition in December, 1975–January, 1976, as a U.S. Bicentennial event. The grave of De Anza was discovered some years ago in the cathedral of Arizpe, Mexico. The scapular that was found with his bones showed that he had been a Franciscan tertiary.

12. Bolton IV, 91–93.

13. Bolton IV, 94 ff.

14. Bolton IV, 110.

15. Bolton IV, 111.

16. Bolton IV, 118 ff.

17. Bolton IV, 115.

18. Bolton IV, 120 ff.

19. Bolton IV, 125 ff.

20. Bolton IV, 124 ff. Geiger II, 140–41, discusses the problem of what constitutes official foundation of a mission. Foundation occurs, it seems, whenever the priests conducting the ceremonies at the mission location intend it to occur.

21. Geiger II, 142, 145.

22. Bolton IV, 159 ff.

23. Bolton IV, 166–68.

5/Under Governor Neve (1777-82)

Despite such internal squabbles, by January, 1777, Spain had achieved most of her initial objectives in Alta California. True, she held only a narrow strip of coast stretching from San Diego to San Francisco, but in these two ports she controlled the best harbors, and in Monterey between them a feasible roadstead. At all three places she possessed a garrisoned presidio supported by a mission only a few miles away. Her eight missions scattered up and down the coastline had under instruction many hundreds of Indians, and were rapidly expanding. Besides, civilian pueblos were spreading around the presidios. She had sent ships north of San Francisco to see whether other good harbors remained unclaimed up there and they had found none south of the Columbia River. No threat appeared on the horizon save possibly from occasional foreign ships which sometimes entered Pacific waters. As the missionaries kept reminding the government in Mexico City the main task now was to strengthen the mission chain, especially along the Santa Barbara Channel where thousands of Chumash Indians awaited conversion to Christianity and education in Spanish ways.

At Christmastime, 1776, Viceroy Bucareli wrote to Fr. Serra that establishment of three missions along that Channel stood next in the program.[1] If Fr. Serra would inform the viceroy what supplies would be needed to set them up, he would obtain them and see that they were transported to Alta California to be ready on demand. Simultaneously Bucareli ordered Neve, the newly appointed governor, to help Fr. Serra prepare for at least two missions, to be dedicated to San Buenaventura and the Immaculate Conception of Mary. So on his way northward from Loreto, where he had been acting as lieutenant-governor, Neve studied the Channel as he rode along it. Reaching Monterey on February 3, 1777, he took over the governorship from Rivera. And on June 3 he wrote to the viceroy a report recommending three missions for the Channel: one at Asumpta on its eastern end (San Buenaventura); another at La Espada at its western extremity near Point Concepción; a third and largest at Mescaltitán in the present Goleta area, under the patronage of Santa Barbara. A presidio should be fortified near the latter, Neve urged.[2]

Fr. Serra soon discovered that Governor Neve was a cold, secretive man who refused to regard the Franciscan missions in Alta California as true missions. For him they were *doctrinas*, or parish-like places of instruction, under the jurisdiction not of the College of San Fernando but of some bishop in Mexico, either the bishop of Durango or the bishop of Guadalajara, though Neve was clever enough never to specify which one.[3] This was an unheard of proposition for the California missionaries, and one, moreover, which sought to separate them from the guidance and help of their superiors at the college.

If Bucareli had retained his powers over the governor of California, Neve might never have tried this gambit. But a reorganization took place in the distribution of powers within the administration of the Mexican provinces. On January 14, 1778, the viceroy ruefully informed Fr. Serra that California no longer lay under his jurisdiction. By a royal decree in Madrid the northern provinces of New Spain (including Nueva Vizcaya, Coahuila, Sinaloa, Sonora, New Mexico, Texas, and California) had been combined into a separate political entity to be called Provincias Internas, with its capital at Arizpe.[4] Over it as commandant general ruled Teodoro de Croix, nephew of the former viceroy, Carlos de Croix. This arrangement substituted for a civilian viceroy a military man far less sympathetic to Franciscan ideas of the prime importance of Christian conversion of the natives. The missionaries lost the friendly help of Bucareli, while Governor Neve served under a man after his own heart.

This combination of circumstances impeded the founding of additional missions so badly that no others could be erected until 1782. Furthermore, it even threatened to deprive Fr. Serra of his faculty to administer the sacrament of confirmation to Indians already baptized at the missions. In the absence of any bishop in California Fr. Serra had applied to the pope in 1774 for the right to administer this sacrament for ten years. After being held up in Madrid for four years in order that the king and his Council of the Indies might approve, it at last reached Fr. Serra on June 17, 1778, in the form of a written *patente.* He immediately made use of the faculty at Mission San Carlos, took ship for San Diego, and traveled slowly north administering the sacrament mission by mission during the autumn of 1778. All this without any comment from Governor Neve. But when Fr. Serra on September 12, 1779, asked the governor for a guard to accompany him to Mission Santa Clara and Mission San Francisco for the same purpose, Neve refused. Said Neve, the *patente* in Fr. Serra's possession did not bear the king's written approval (*pase*) and, without that, was void according to a decree issued by the king himself on November 23, 1777.[5]

Fr. Serra naturally regarded Neve's objection as a gross interference with a religious authority conferred by the pope himself. But in order to meet the governor on his own ground he maintained that the original copy of the *patente,* kept by his college in its archives in Mexico City, must have borne the royal *pase,* for the college would never have sent him an illegal permit. On that argument he gave overt obedience to Neve's veto but went on confirming surreptitiously. Nevertheless he wrote both to the college and to the viceroy's office asking them to inspect the original document and to make affidavits that it bore the king's approval, if such was the case, as he was sure it must be. By the end of 1780 this inspection had been completed, the royal signature verified, and assurances to that effect sent to both Governor Neve and Commander de Croix. By August 16, 1781, Fr. Serra had letters from both men that he could proceed with his confirmations.[6] This futile controversy had interfered with mission confirmations for over a year. Fr. Serra, however, made up for lost time by visiting and confirming at all his missions twice more before he died in 1784.

Ever since the founding of Mission Santa Clara early in 1777, Fr. Serra had been writing letters to his college in Mexico City, to the viceroy, and to the commandante of the Internal Provinces pleading that he be authorized to set up missions along the Channel. The imminence of war between Spain and England in late 1778, leading up to its outbreak on June 23, 1779, no doubt was a factor that worked powerfully in his favor. The thought of what the British navy might do along the undefended channel coast could not have been comfortable to contemplate. Consequently, late in 1778 Teodoro de Croix proposed to Viceroy Martín de Mayoraga that a presidio and three missions be established in that area, to be named "San Buenaventura, Santa Barbara, and Purísima Concepción." The viceroy assented, and asked the College of San Fernando for six friars to staff the three missions. Fr. Serra likewise wrote to the college with the same request on April 6, 1779.[7]

Anza's precedent of recruiting married soldiers and settlers for the San Francisco settlements had worked so well
that it was used again in 1780 for the Channel establishments. This time former governor Rivera, now reduced to
captain, received orders to recruit and lead the expedition.[8]
Rivera managed to gather 14 settler families and 59 soldiers,
many of them married. Their pack train consisted of nearly
1000 head of cattle, horses, and mules. They rendezvoused
at Alamos in Sonora, where Rivera divided them into two
more or less equal groups, one to travel north by land
through Baja California under Lt. José de Zúñiga, the other
to take Anza's overland trail through the land of the Yuma
Indians under Rivera's own leadership.

Both parties left Alamos in the spring of 1781 but their
fates differed. Zúñiga's group reached Mission San Gabriel
in mid-August without loss of life. Having arrived early in
July among the Yumas, hitherto friendly to the Spaniards,
Rivera decided that his pack animals needed a rest. He sent
on along the westward trail some 35 men with families
under an escort of nine soldiers, while he himself remained
behind with the pack animals and the remaining soldiers
to guard them. Those who went ahead made it safely to
Mission San Gabriel on July 14, 1781. Rivera and his
companions who stayed behind were slaughtered to the
last man by the Yumas, who also destroyed two missions
and killed four missionaries within their borders. From then
on, the overland route through Yuma territory could no
longer be depended upon as a link with Alta California.
Commerce with Mexico for many years moved solely by sea.

Despite their losses among the Yumas the great majority
of Rivera's recruits had arrived safely at Mission San Gabriel
by the end of August, 1781. It happened that Governor
Neve spent nearly a year in 1781–1782 at that same mission,

attending to a pet project of his own, the foundation of the pueblo which we now call Los Angeles.[9] Some 48 of the new arrivals from Rivera's expedition chose to live in the pueblo, which they gave a name in honor of the Blessed Virgin Mary: Nuestra Señora Reina de los Angeles de Por-ciúncula (Our Lady Queen of the Angels at Portiuncula). As noted earlier (p. 14) the popular tongue, with its usual impatience for long names, has since abbreviated this to Los Angeles, thereby taking away the pueblo from our Lady and giving it to her angels.

Franciscans had nothing to do with the founding of this pueblo. To Fr. Serra every such pueblo in Alta California was premature and a potential threat to the right conversion of Indians. Late in 1781 he had received permission both military and religious to set up at long last the three Channel missions. The obvious base of operations for such a project was Mission San Gabriel, which was close to the Channel and which now also harbored Governor Neve and a large number of soldiers and colonists. Fr. Serra and Fr. Cambón consequently went there, and were ready and waiting when Neve left the mission on March 26, 1782 (Tuesday of Holy Week), to go to Asumpta to found Mission San Buenaventura. The governor had with him besides the two priests an extraordinarily large column led by Sgt. Ortega, consisting of 80 soldiers and their families, some Christian Indians, muleteers, and a train of cattle and pack animals loaded with church goods and utensils for house and field.[10]

Scarcely had this party left Mission San Gabriel when a messenger from Captain Fages caught up with them to ask the governor to consult with Fages about launching a puni-tive force against the Yumas. Neve then returned to the mission to talk to Fages, but Sgt. Ortega led the rest of the expedition on to Asumpta, arriving on March 29 or 30. After inspecting the site carefully, Fr. Serra founded Mission

San Buenaventura Mission (founded 1782), in 1903 (top), and in 1975 (bottom).

San Buenaventura there on March 31, 1782, Easter morning.[11] He raised and blessed the cross, sang high Mass at an altar inside a brushwood shelter, and preached. Then they all pitched in to build a chapel and living quarters for the priests and guard, the whole surrounded by a stockade. Neve rejoined them there eleven days after the founding.

So, at last, San Buenaventura had his mission in one of the most populous regions along the Channel. This great Franciscan (1221–1274), who combined humble personal piety with one of the towering intellects of the Middle Ages, was venerated by Franciscans ever after, not only for his theological writings, but also for his abilities as an administrator, which saved the Order from division and collapse after the death of St. Francis, its founder. San Buenaventura was elected its head in 1257, and held that office for seventeen years. He came to be venerated as virtually the second founder of the Order. Small wonder that the Franciscan missionaries in California had chafed under the delay of thirteen years since 1769 in giving him a mission worthy of his importance.

Governor Neve's absence had allowed Fr. Serra to establish Mission San Buenaventura in the manner of the Franciscan mission system. The agreement between the two men was that the founding of that mission would be followed immediately by the founding of the Mission and Presidio of Santa Barbara. Accordingly, on April 15, 1782, they left a soldier guard at Mission San Buenaventura (nowadays shortened to Ventura) and proceeded together some ten leagues northwest to what Fr. Crespi had named Laguna de la Concepción, presumably because of the nearness to the present Point Conception.[12] Here Neve insisted that the Presidio of Santa Barbara be founded before the mission. Fr. Serra acceded. Inasmuch as the six missionaries requested from the college for the Channel missions had not arrived, and Fr. Serra had had to leave his sole companion, Fr. Cambón, at Mission San Buenaventura, he had to officiate alone.

On April 21, 1782, (feast of the Patronage of St. Joseph), Fr. Serra blessed the soil, erected and blessed a cross, sang a "low" (not solemn) Mass, and preached.[13] In conclusion all present sang the *Alabado.* Inscribing the church registers Fr. Serra called the new foundation "this New Mission and Royal Presidio of Santa Barbara." He dedicated it, he wrote, to "Santa Barbara, virgin and martyr, on the land of Yamnonalit. I was and am alone, and therefore the holy Mass was a low Mass, and in place of *Te Deum* we had the *Alabado,* which is the equivalent of the *Laudamus.* May God bless it. Amen." Fr. Serra felt sure that the mission-presidio combination was only temporary and that Neve would go ahead with his agreement to found a separate mission. Three weeks of waiting dragged on but the governor gave no sign of intending to build anything more.

When reproached by Fr. Serra Neve answered that he would not allow the foundation of a mission unless it conformed to his idea of what a mission ought to be—in effect merely a parish church to serve the presidio and nearby Indian tribes, who were to remain domiciled in their home villages. This was the old enemy again, the conception of mission work which Franciscans had been fighting since Sierra Gorda days, and before. In their view the genuine conversion of the Indians and their training for a useful role in civil life could not be accomplished under Neve's kind of system. Fr. Serra found the governor adamant. Whereupon he departed, leaving the mission unfounded.

Notes

1. Geiger, *Serra* II, 145–46.

2. Geiger II, 150.

3. Geiger II, 159–63.

4. Geiger II, 152–53.

5. Geiger II, 184 ff. On that date the king Carlos III of Spain issued a decree that all papal briefs, before taking effect in his territories, must have both his own royal *pase* and that of the viceroy or his delegate enjoying the *real patronato* (royal patronage) in the diocese where the papal brief was to be used. Neve claimed that he had the right to the *real patronato* and consequently the power to challenge Fr. Serra's papal brief of confirmation unless it bore all the necessary *pases*. A peculiar power of veto, from our point of view.

6. Geiger II, 226–33.

7. Geiger II, 283–84.

8. Geiger II, 268 ff.; Bolton, *Historical Memoirs* IV, 207–10.

9. Geiger II, 266–73.

10. Geiger II, 286–87; Bolton IV, 210 ff.

11. Bolton IV, 212.

12. Geiger II, 287.

13. Bolton IV, 214; Geiger II, 288; Engelhardt, *Missions and Missionaries* II, 369. "Yamnonalit" or "Yanonalit" was the chief of a tribe of friendly Indians near the new presidio. This fact opens up the possibility that many, or all, of the Indian names similarly mentioned in the founding of the missions are in fact the names of local chiefs, not of tribes or districts.

6/Under Governor Fages, Second Term (1782-90) Death of Fr. Serra (1784) Fr. Lasuén's First Missions (1784-91)

Between this episode and his death some two years afterwards Fr. Serra kept on touring his missions from time to time in order to administer confirmations, but he was too ill and too preoccupied with dangers threatening from the outside even to try to add to their numbers. One cause of his preoccupation came from Bishop Reyes' attempts from 1780 on to break down the Franciscan mission system on the grounds that it encouraged missionaries to defy authority and to treat their Indian converts like slaves under the lash.[1]

To simplify a long story, Reyes persuaded the king to make him bishop (with the pope's consent) over a new diocese comprising the provinces of Sonora, Sinaloa, and both Californias. His plan was to set up in those four provinces four "custodies" or groups of friaries of missionaries in the regions where they worked. These he designed to run according to his own notions quite independently of the mother houses of the Orders to which they belonged. In short, on the pretext of more local control over the missionaries, leading ostensibly to more humane treatment of Indian converts, he wanted to substitute himself for the colleges from which the missionaries came. Reyes' scheme foundered on lack of money to support the "custodies" and on refusal of the friars to become disloyal to their colleges. The king withdrew his backing of the Reyes plan in 1791, after loud complaints reached him, not only from the colleges, but also from some friars who had originally been drawn into the "custodies." No such machinery was ever set up in Alta California, but the distinct possibility that it might well be introduced helped to trouble Fr. Serra's last years.

An even more alarming possibility arose in 1783 when Fr. Hidalgo, president of the Dominican missionaries in Baja California, persuaded Bishop Reyes to recommend that Dominicans should replace Franciscans in the missions of Alta California.[2] Bishop Reyes was all too persuadable. He wrote a recommendation to that effect to Commander Neve of the Internal Provinces on December 13, 1783. Surprisingly enough, Neve retorted on December. 29 with a letter warmly praising the achievements of the Franciscan missions in Alta California. Nor did he agree that the Dominicans had displayed any great success in their Baja California missions. This stand effectually killed the Dominican scheme. But for many months Fr. Serra did not know this, and spent great effort trying to resign himself and his colleagues to being displaced from the missions in which they had long labored. The danger disappeared, however, and a weary Fr. Serra could die in peace on August 28, 1784.

His successor as president of the missions, Fr. Fermin de Lasuen, had at first shown much discontent with his lot as a missionary but had developed into an able administrator who possessed the valuable faculty of being liked. Fortunately for him, before he took office Neve had been promoted to commander of the Internal Provinces, and in his place as governor of California appeared none other than an older and wiser Pedro Fages, determined not to repeat the mistakes of his first tenure of that office. Late in 1783 Fages and Fr. Vicente de Santa María had explored the vicinity of the Santa Barbara presidio for an eligible mission site and had found one at Montecito, on the eastern outskirts of the present city of Santa Barbara.[3] On April 1, 1784, Neve as commander of Internal Provinces approved the Montecito site and even charged Fages to be sure that the land selected was "to the satisfaction of the religious." A year later Viceroy Matías de Gálvez repeated the order, and most important of all, made 1000 pesos from the Pious Fund available for the projected Mission Santa Barbara. This financial assurance in turn seems to have encouraged six volunteers from the College of San Fernando to commit themselves in 1786 as missionaries for the three Channel establishments, not only for the already flourishing Mission San Buenaventura but for Mission Santa Barbara and Mission Purísima Concepción, which were still in the planning stage.

In these circumstances Fr. Lasuen had time to shake down into his new duties without facing immediately any problem more serious than the founding of two channel missions. For these all the requisite equipment was already in hand. Towards the end of 1786, therefore, he traveled south from Monterey with Frs. Oramas and Paterna. Fr. Lasuén was the sort of man who liked to examine proposed sites with his own eyes. He concluded that the Montecito site for Mission Santa Barbara was unsatisfactory, and chose instead a spot known locally as El Pedregoso (The Strong Place) considerably closer to the presidio, in fact only about half a league northwest of it. Evidently, whether wisely or unwisely, Fr. Lasuén did not share Fr. Serra's alarm at the proximity of a presidio to a mission.

On the afternoon of December 4, 1786, the feast day of Santa Barbara, Virgin and Martyr, he raised and blessed a great cross at El Pedregoso.[4] But he courteously awaited the coming of governor Fages on December 14 before accomplishing the formal rites of foundation for Mission Santa Barbara. Also on the presidio books Fr. Lasuen changed Fr. Serra's "Mission and Royal Presidio" inscription to "Esta Nuevo Real Presidio" (This New Royal Presidio), thus officially separating the mission from the presidio.

Santa Barbara was one of those Christian women who died in defense of their chastity at an indefinite date in early Roman times (third century?). The mission obviously took her for its patron saint chiefly because the Channel on which it was situated had long been named after her. The naming of several of the Channel islands after other virgin martyrs has already been noted. Also influential, probably, was the nearness of all these places to Point Conception, referring to the Immaculate Conception of the Blessed Virgin Mary, that is, her conception free from the taint of Original Sin. This, in turn, led to the naming of the mission soon to be started near the Point as Purísima Concepción, in honor of our Lady. With the patronage of Santa Inés (Saint Agnes), one of the most venerated of the chaste Roman virgin martyrs, over Mission Santa Inés in 1804 the specialization of this little group of missions in virgin saints was confirmed and completed.

Ever since December, 1780, at the latest, Viceroy Martín de Mayorga had been writing letters coupling plans for setting up a Mission Purísima Concepción with plans for setting up Mission San Buenaventura and Mission Santa Barbara. By the end of the year 1786 the latter two had come into existence, as just described. Moreover the tireless Governor Fages had already made preliminary examination of what Fr. Lasuén described, in a letter of August 12, 1786, as "the place mistakenly called La Gaviota, but in reality Santa Rosa, for the purpose of founding La Purísima

Santa Barbara Mission (founded 1786), in 1903 (top), and in 1975 (bottom).

Mission there."[5] And Fages had issued a friendly invitation to Fr. Lasuén to join him next spring (1787) in looking over the ground. Fr. Lasuén had gladly accepted.

Presumably this joint examination was duly made in the spring, for near the end of 1787 Fr. Lasuén took with him Fr. Fuster and Fr. Arriota to the south bank of the Santa Rosa River (now called the Santa Inés River). At a place where the town of Lompoc now stands they founded Mission Purísima Concepción with all due rites on December 8, 1786.[6] Unfortunately, after the shattering 1812 earthquake the mission had to be entirely relocated and rebuilt four miles to the north and east in the little valley of Los Berros. As always the full name Fr. Lasuén gave it at its inception is revealing: "La Misión de la Purísima Concepción de la Santísima Virgen María, Madre de Dios y Nuestra Señora" (The Mission of the Immaculate Conception of the Most Holy Virgin Mary, Mother of God, and Our Lady). This full title shows beyond all doubt, that the conception referred to is that of the Virgin Mary unspotted by Original Sin, not of her bearing of a sinless Christ. As in other mission titles, devotion to Mary and praise of her attributes are much more explicit here than in the popular abbreviation of the name to Mission Purísima Concepción, which seems vague by comparison. Colorless and uninformative also is the mere specification in many recent histories of the date of foundation as December 8. Fr. Lasuén's own full inscription in the mission's Book of Baptisms reveals why he chose December 8 as the founding date: ". . . begun on the auspicious feast of the singularly Most Pure Mystery of the Heavenly Empress, Mary Most Holy, that is to say, her Immaculate Conception. Saturday, December 8, 1787." That is, Fr. Lasuén piously waited for the feast of the Immaculate Conception.[7]

In summary, then, by the close of 1787 the mission chain

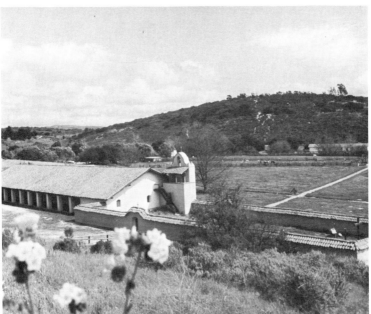

La Purísima Concepción Mission (founded 1787), in 1903 (top), and in 1975 (bottom).

79

had acquired three missions along the channel and closed the long gap which had previously stretched between Mission San Gabriel and Mission San Luis Obispo. From both a missionary and a military point of view there remained the task of strengthening the provincial capital at Monterey by giving Mission San Carlos Borromeo de Carmelo closer companions to its north and south. In this instance the first impetus in this development came from the College of San Fernando in Mexico City, which wrote to Viceroy Manuel Antonio Flores on September 22, 1789, proposing two more missions near Monterey.[8]

A change in the viceroyalty was occurring just then with the ascension of the Conde de Rivella Gigedo to that office on October 17 of the same year. The latter lost no time in accepting the college's request. In a letter of October 31, 1789, he replied to the guardian of the college: "Agreeing to the proposition which Your Reverence makes . . . I have resolved that two missions should be established in New California, one in the valley of Soledad close to the Río de Monterey (Salinas River) between the mission of San Antonio and that of San Carlos, and the other between the missions of San Carlos and Santa Clara, about twenty-five leagues distant from the former on the spot called Santa Cruz." For these two he promised the usual foundation stipend of 1000 pesos each from the Pious Fund, and asked the college to provide four missionaries. With the beginning of the French Revolution in 1789 the times were growing troubled. It looks as if the viceroy was more than ever anxious to consolidate the Spanish position around Monterey.

In the same letter of October 31, 1789, anticipating future needs, he also requested that the missionaries should try to discover "suitable localities between San Diego and San Juan Capistrano, San Gabriel and San Buenaventura in order to fill the gaps with intermediate missions . . ."[9] Such establish-

Santa Cruz Mission (founded 1791), in 1903 (top), and in 1975 (bottom).

ments would strengthen the southern flank of the mission chain. But clearly they were only to be explored for, not founded yet. The two missions at Santa Cruz and Soledad were to be built as soon as possible in locations already known and chosen.

Santa Cruz (Holy Cross), strategically situated near the north end of Monterey Bay, had been so named by Fr. Crespi in his diary of the first Portolá expedition on October 18, 1769, and its excellence in water, wood, and fertile land enthusiastically described. Preparing to found a mission there as ordered, Fr. Lasuén discovered that the trickle of supplies sent him for the purpose was thinning, probably because of the revolutionary upheavals in Europe. On January 20, 1791, the viceroy ordered him to get all possible help from already established missions, and on July 22 Fr. Lasuén sent them a plea for loans and donations.[10] Five of his missions responded with what gifts they could spare in the form of vestments and sacred vessels. The frigate *Aranzazu* arrived shortly afterwards with a "dowry" of other supplies. Using Mission Santa Clara as a base camp, Fr. Lasuén himself crossed the intervening hills by a "very long and very rough" road and found the proposed site "just as beautiful and just as suitable as had been reported to me. I came upon a channel of water close at hand, very plentiful, and very essential."[11]

Consequently, on the feast of St. Augustine, August 28, 1791, he said Mass there, planted the cross, blessed it, and dedicated the mission to the Holy Cross. Most pleasing it was to Fr. Lasuén, that during the ceremonies many Indians appeared who gave evidence of wanting "to enroll themselves under the sacred standard." The two immediate needs, as Fr. Lasuén saw them, were to build huts for residences and to improve the road to the new mission so that the supplies could be brought in. For these works he enlisted the help of Indian converts from Mission Santa Clara, and also of the commander of the San Francisco presidio with some of his men. Leaving these construction projects well under way, Fr. Lasuén returned to Mission Santa Clara. Why Fr. Crespi had named this particular spot Santa Cruz in the first instance is not altogether clear, aside from the paramount fact that Christ redeemed the world by His Crucifixion. In every one of the Stations of the Cross, especially revered by Franciscans, Jesus is thanked because "by Your Holy Cross You have redeemed the world." The same name marked dozens of places of all kinds throughout Spanish America, including that of the Franciscan mother college of Santa Cruz de Querétaro, about 125 miles northwest of Mexico City.

At Mission Santa Clara Fr. Lasuén next proceeded to organize the expedition which would found the mission at Soledad.[12] Its precise location was so well fixed in advance that he sent ahead to it "eleven Indians . . . with a supply of implements to build a hut at Soledad so that we may accommodate the missionaries and the supplies." Fr. Lasuén also notified the padres at the neighboring missions of San Luis Obispo and San Antonio to "make other preparations" for the founding ceremonies, by which he probably meant that they should oversee the construction of the buildings and be present with the necessary religious goods. He planned to arrive there himself, he wrote to them, "at the latest, immediately after the feast of Saint Francis" (October 4). As good as his word, Fr. Lasuén came in time to dedicate the mission on October 9, 1791, with the help of Fr. Diego García and Fr. Mariano Rubí. The name he gave it is significant: "Mission of Mary Most Holy, Nuestra Señora de Soledad, called by the natives Chutusgalis, but ever since the recent entrada into that country known by our people as La Soledad."[13] It is situated in the Salinas Valley, near the present King City.

The name *Soledad* for this spot in the Salinas Valley has had a strange history and, to those who know Catholic theology, concealed meanings. It does not appear anywhere in that region in Fr. Crespi's diary of 1769. Nevertheless, Fr. Font recorded in his diary of 1776 that the name had in fact been used first by the soldiers of the 1769 expedition at that spot.[14] The story, as told to Fr. Font by the soldiers of his own expedition, was that the 1769 soldiers had there met with a single Indian man and asked his name. Since his mumbled reply sounded to them like "Soledad" they gave that name both to him and to the place where they camped that night. For them it seems to have had no great religious significance.

Fr. Serra, however, told a different and more believable story.[15] When he was returning to Monterey in July, 1771, after founding Mission San Antonio de Padua, several Indian women approached his camp. One of them, when Fr. Serra asked her name, answered with a word that sounded to him like the Spanish word "Soledad." Turning to his companions Fr. Serra exclaimed, "Here you have María de la Soledad" (Mary of Solitude). The Mary he meant was the Blessed Virgin, and the Solitude to which he referred was her lonely grief at the time of the Crucifixion of her Son. Spanish-speaking countries of the eighteenth century practised a special form of Marian devotion on Holy Saturday of Passion Week to commemorate Mary's unspeakable aloneness and sorrow during the hours between the Crucifixion and Resurrection of Jesus. By attaching Mary's name to La Soledad Fr. Serra was transforming Soledad from a description of the physical desolation of the place into the spiritual desolation felt by our Lady. He was well acquainted with the special Marian devotions of Holy Week, having taking part in them at the College of San Fernando. And

Nuestra Señora de la Soledad Mission (founded 1791), in 1903 (top), and in 1975 (bottom).

Fr. Serra's church at Jalpan in the Sierra Gorda had a statue of Mary holding a crown of thorns, "probably representing Our Lady of Solitude," thinks Fr. Geiger. Fr. Lasuén's naming the mission at Soledad for "Mary Most Holy, Nuestra Señora de la Soledad" adopts the same tradition. Those who reduce the name of the mission to "Soledad" today are demolishing or concealing this religious meaning.

Notes

1. Geiger, *Serra* II, 344 ff. and 354 ff.

2. Geiger II, 367 ff.

3. Finbar Kenneally, *Writings of Fermín Francisco de Lasuén,* 2 vols. (Washington, D.C.: Academy of American Franciscan History, 1965), I, 100-01; Engelhardt, *Missions and Missionaries* II, 432-33.

4. Kenneally I, 144 ff.; Engelhardt II, 433-34.

5. Kenneally I, 139; Engelhardt II, 434-35. The reference to La Gaviota is to Crespi's diary entry for August 24, 1769, describing how the name derived from the soldiers' killing a seagull at that spot. See Bolton II, 158.

6. Engelhardt II, 435.

7. J. S. Chase and C. F. Saunders, *The California Padres and Their Missions* (Houghton Mifflin, 1915), pp. 188, 208; Kenneally II, 433.

8. Engelhardt II, 452 ff.

9. Engelhardt II, 452.

10. Engelhardt II, 453; Kenneally I, 225 ff.

11. Kenneally I, 235 ff.

12. Kenneally I, 235.

13. Engelhardt II, 454.

14. Bolton, *Historical Memoirs* IV, 287, under date of March 9, 1776.

15. Geiger I, 281.

7/Searches for More Sites;
Missions of 1797

After dedicating the missions at Santa Cruz and Soledad in 1791, Fr. Lasuén founded no others in Alta California until 1797, six years later.[1] Inasmuch as Spain and Revolutionary France were warring with each other from 1793 to 1795, the interval cannot have been propitious for the commitment of further Spanish resources to California. But in obedience to the viceroy's aforementioned letter of October, 1789, Fr. Lasuén kept his missionaries looking for potential new mission sites, especially between San Diego and San Juan Capistrano, and between San Gabriel and San Buenaventura. The Marqués de Branciforte, coming to the viceroyalty in 1794, and Diego de Borica to the governorship of California in the same year, did nothing to discourage exploration. Indeed, by the middle of 1795 Governor Borica kept urging Fr. Lasuén to order his priests in the already established foundations to extend their search for sites all the way from San Diego to San Francisco.[2]

In a letter dated November 28, 1795, Fr. Lasuén reported to his superiors at the College of San Fernando that Governor Borica wanted pinpointing of locations for as many as five new missions.7 Two were to be between San Diego and San Buenaventura as originally proposed, a third between

89

San Luis Obispo and San Antonio de Padua, a fourth between San Carlos and Santa Clara, a fifth between Santa Clara and San Francisco. At the time of writing, Fr. Lasuén went on, he had already dispatched four expeditions under local missionaries into the five regions specified, and had so far received written reports from all the expeditions save one, that led by Fr. Dantí from the San Francisco Bay area. When all the documents had come in, Fr. Lasuén drew up from them a summary memorandum, which he entitled *Notes on Projected Foundations*, dated January 12, 1796. This memorandum included his own personal comments on the findings submitted.[3]

Normal procedure would have been for Governor Borica to submit to higher authority a request for the five missions as originating from him. He thought it would be more persuasive, however, for Fr. Lasuén to draw up the request as if originating from the missionaries and send it to the governor, who would then forward it to Mexico City. Fr. Lasuén preferred not to sponsor the request, since it had not in fact begun with the missionaries but with Borica. The latter, consequently, did submit the proposal for the five missions to Viceroy Branciforte on February 26, 1796, along with Fr. Lasuén's *Notes*. This little episode shows that it was primarily Governor Borica who desired the new missions, probably in order to afford California more protection from sudden landing by the increasing numbers of foreign ships.

Viceroy Branciforte proceeded to get from the College of San Fernando assurances that ten missionaries were available to staff five missions.[4] He also arranged for the usual financial support from the Pious Fund for the whole project: 1000 pesos for the foundation of each mission, 400 pesos annually for each missionary. The college then asked the viceroy to indicate a titular saint for each of the five missions. On November 14 Branciforte chose San Miguel Arcángel, San Fernando Rey de Espana, San Carlos Borromeo, San Antonio de Padua, and San Luis Rey de Francia. He seemed totally unaware that San Carlos and San Antonio had long had California missions under their patronage. This oversight is hard to explain on any grounds creditable to Branciforte, who had then been in office for nearly two years. When informed of his error by the college, he substituted the names of San José and San Juan Bautista (St. John the Baptist) in place of those of the two saints already provided with missions.[5] He did not, however, attach the name of any saint to any particular mission. That detail he left to Fr. Lasuén and Governor Borica.

The Napoleonic wars were now in full swing. News of peace with formidable France reached California on March 5, 1796, but within a year came news that Spain had fallen into a war with Britain, potentially still more dangerous to California coastal establishments because of its predominance in sea power. Borica was more anxious than ever to inaugurate the five new missions, the missing links, and pressed Fr. Lasuén hard to found them all in the single year, 1797. Never since the California missions began back in 1769 had more than two been founded in any one year. That he should be asked to found five struck Fr. Lasuén as monstrous and impossible. He privately lamented the governor's precipitancy but promised at least to do his best.

On April 14, 1797, arrival at San Francisco of the ten missionaries promised by the College of San Fernando for assignment to the five missions sounded the summons to action for Fr. Lasuén.[6] He decided to begin in the north with the founding of Mission San José and to work southwards successively to San Juan Bautista, San Miguel, San Fernando Rey de España and San Luis Rey de Francia in that order. He would use so far as possible the geographical data collected for him by the four expeditions he had sent out in 1795. Much of their data, he suspected, would prove unreliable and inexact. So he anticipated having to do a good deal of re-exploration himself on the sites recommended.

Before Fr. Lasuén could even begin the new foundations he was shocked to receive word on April 29 that a pueblo to be named Villa Branciforte after the viceroy was to be placed, to use his own words, "within a distance of three or four gunshots of Santa Cruz Mission. This is the greatest misfortune that has ever befallen mission lands."[7] Fr. Lasuén considered plantation of a pueblo so close to Mission Santa Cruz a plain violation of the Law of the Indies promulgated in Madrid, and he foresaw for Mission Santa Cruz all the troubles usually arising from the proximity of a town. Worst of all, he was commanded by the viceroy to help the new pueblo by every means at his disposal, including food supplies, in the very year when he must put five missions into operation, which would likewise need food and every other kind of supply before they could get on their feet. Supplies from Mexico to California were slowing to a trickle because so much had to be shipped in the other direction to war-torn Spain. Fr. Lasuén's protests went unheeded. He could not even get a ruling about priorities as between Villa Branciforte and the five additional missions expected of him. Under these circumstances he tended to give preference to the missions.

The northernmost exploration led by Sergeant Pedro Amador and Fr. Dantí under instructions to find a good mission site between Missions San Francisco and Santa Clara had spotted one which they thought ideal in November, 1796. It lay "about seven or eight leagues to the north from Santa Clara" but on the east side of the Bay near the Arroyo de Alameda almost across from Mission Dolores. Fr. Dantí had erected a cross on a slight elevation which he named San Francisco Solano after the Franciscan friar (1549-1610)

San José de Guadalupe Mission (founded 1797), in 1903 (top), and in 1975 (bottom).

who had done extraordinary work among the Indians of Tucuman (Argentina). [8]

Fr. Lasuén may have gone to look over this location himself. In any case he approved it as "a very suitable site for a mission, despite the fact that it is somewhat short of firewood and lumber." On June 9, 1797, therefore, he went there from Mission Santa Clara, accompanied by a body of soldiers under Sgt. Amador and by Frs. Isidoro Barcenilla and Agustín Merino, who were to be in charge of the mission. San Francisco Solano was not on the viceroy's list of patron saints, however. St. Joseph was. So when Fr. Lasuén founded the mission on June 11, the feast of the Holy Trinity, he dedicated it to "the Most Glorious Patriarch St. Joseph, the fosterfather of Our Lord." [9] In the usual ceremonies the priests blessed water, earth, and a cross, and sang the Mass together. From its beginnings in 1769 the whole California enterprise had been put under the protection of this saint. Now, belatedly, San José had a mission dedicated in his honor.

Surely not altogether without design, Mission San José had a highly strategic location. For one thing it helped control the east side of the Bay opposite the peninsula. For another it stood astride a pass leading inland to the San Joaquín valley, long used by the natives of the interior valleys for access to San Francisco Bay. In fact they were starting to use it to make raids on the mule trains going to and from the town of San José and the missions of the Bay area.

Mission San José thus became an ambiguous cross between a religious establishment for the saving of souls and a military post for subduing hostile men. From it Spanish troops could and did launch fairly frequent punitive or preventive sweeps of the interior, or raids to recover fugitives from the missions. On July 10, 1797, for example, only a month after the mission was founded, Sgt. Amador led an expedition against the Cuchillones and Scalenes which brought back more than 80 runaways from several missions, as well as nine chiefs from the tribes which harbored them. Other Spanish expeditions of the same sort in 1805 and 1826 produced large-scale fighting. In the intervals Fr. Durán and Fr. Fortuni worked hard and ably to make Mission San José a genuine religious foundation, but obviously the handicaps were severe. The fact is that the tribes in the interior never were subdued, and the majority of them did not relish conversion.

While exploring in November, 1795, for a fitting site for a mission between Monterey and Santa Clara, Fr. Dantí had seen two possibilities, one on the San Benito, near its source, the other on the upper reaches of the Río Pájaro in San Bernardino valley near present-day Gilroy.[10] The latter was some 12 leagues from Mission Santa Clara and about 14 from Mission San Carlos. The San Benito site, on the other hand, stood some 11 leagues from San Carlos and 14 or 15 from Santa Clara. After reading Fr. Dantí's journal, Fr. Lasuén determined that if the two sites proved to be equally good, the one which offered the best prospects for the conversion of the largest number of natives should be chosen.

Early in 1797 Fr. Lasuén had made up his mind in favor of the San Benito site for Mission San Juan Bautista. Indeed, on the very day of his founding Mission San José (June 11), he wrote to Governor Borica that the situation for the next new mission to the south had already been marked out. More, he ordered the building of a number of huts at San Benito to provide shelter for the missionaries and for the supplies gathered for their mission.[11]

One factor in particular called for speed in these preparations. The feast day of San Juan Bautista, to whom the mission was to be dedicated, fell on June 24. Founding the saint's mission on that day, if possible, was highly desirable.

All the preparations having come off as scheduled, Frs. Lasuén, Pedro Adriano Martínez, and José Manuel de Martiarena came to the site in good time to inaugurate Mission San Juan Bautista formally on June 24. In the presence of crowds of Indian spectators, some pagan, some already converted at other missions, the priests blessed water, earth, and a large standing cross, sang high Mass and the Litany of the Saints and the *Te Deum*. Fr. Lasuén in a letter of June 27, 1797, to Governor Borica described the location and the ceremonies, adding "In this manner possession was taken of this region by dedicating it to the glorious Precursor of Our Lord Jesus Christ, St. John the Baptist, thus beginning on his own feast day the mission that bears his holy title." In reporting to Fr. Guardian Pedro Callejas by a letter of June 30, Fr. Lasuén detailed the considerable aid given to the new mission by other missions, a fact which shows that the government authorities in the year 1797 were not shipping to California in full measure the foundation supplies customary for getting new missions under way.

The third of the search expeditions of 1795 had been led by Fr. Buenaventura Sitjar, the veteran from Mission San Antonio de Padua, to survey the ground between that mission and Mission San Luis Obispo.[12] Starting from San Antonio with a band of soldiers Fr. Sitjar explored the Río Nacimiento and the Arroyo de Santa Isabel but found the country mountainous and inhospitable. He then returned to El Camino Real as offering at least flatness and accessibility, and examined the terrain for three leagues on both sides of the highway as far south as Mission San Luis Obispo's *asistencia* at Santa Margarita. In the end the leaders of the expedition saw most promise in a place on the highway itself called Las Pozas (the Waterholes) not far from the Salinas River. Fr. Lasuén's *Notes* of 1796 approved this location as "good

San Juan Bautista Mission (founded 1797), in 1903 (top), and in 1975 (bottom).

from every point of view," being on the main route of travel almost equidistant from San Antonio and San Luis Obispo.[13] Also it had a plentiful source of water in the river nearby to irrigate the fertile fields stretching all around it.

Here, then, on July 25, 1797, the feast day of Santiago (St. James the Greater), the national saint of Spain, Fr. Lasuén gave over the mission to the protection of "the glorious prince, the Archangel St. Michael, in a beautiful region which is called Vahca by the natives."[14] In performing the usual ceremonies he was assisted by Fr. Sitjar, who became Mission San Miguel's first pastor. They were watched by many Salinan Indians.

St. Michael, traditionally the leader of the heavenly armies and first receiver of the souls of the dead, was an apt patron for this mission. It lay due west of the southern end of the San Joaquín valley, called by the Spaniards Tulares (Place of Rushes) from the tules or bulrushes growing in the swamps there. Throughout the mission period hostile non-Christian Indians lived well hidden in that labyrinth, issuing forth from time to time in order to steal mules and horses and to lure away dissatisfied converts. Mission San Miguel served as a buffer against them, and also as a jumping-off place for expeditions of retaliation and exploration.

Fr. Lasuén lingered for a few days at "the incipient Mission of San Miguel," as he called it, resting while he awaited the arrival of supplies for the two additional missions he was still expected to found in 1797: the missions of the kings, San Fernando Rey de España and San Luis Rey de Francia. Writing a letter to the Father Guardian of the college of his Order in Mexico City on July 27 he reported on the uncomfortable midsummer climate at Mission San Miguel, very warm in the day, and still unpleasantly warm even at night: ". . . we all suffer from it for our living quarters are nothing but huts made of branches."[15]

San Miguel Arcángel Mission (founded 1797), in 1903 (top), and in 1975 (bottom).

Four days later he wrote another letter to the Father Guardian complaining passionately that for all of the five missions he was setting up in 1797 "the government is contributing nothing but the six men of the escort. Everything, everything, everything else . . . has to be contributed by the missions, the missionaries, and the Indians. A marvelous achievement, and how little it is appreciated by the civilian government!"[16]   Fr. Lasuén practically never wrote so tempestuously, but his patience was breaking under the severe difficulties of starting five new missions without supplies or equipment except what he could coax out of the thirteen missions already established, all of which suffered from scarcities of their own. To set up five missions in one year would have been a heroic labor of organization and timing under the best of circumstances but to do it virtually alone, without government help or appreciation, sometimes seemed more than Fr. Lasuén could bear. Besides, the Salinas Valley in midsummer was hot enough to discourage anybody. Of course, in the middle of a war the civilian government had its back to the wall, too. Two years later, in 1799, it began putting pressure on all the Calforia missions for cash donations to help Spain in financing the war.

Having founded Mission San Miguel and supervised its first weeks, Fr. Lasuén moved down to Mission Santa Barbara in early August to get ready to establish the two remaining missions. When the mule trains from Monterey reached Santa Barbara bringing the supplies he had collected, he accompanied them down to Mission San Buenaventura at the end of August. There he reorganized the loads into two equal portions, one destined for Mission San Fernando, the other for Mission San Luis Rey. Early in September he started south with the pack train carrying the load for San Fernando, "wishing and hoping to establish it on the eighth

San Fernando Rey de España Mission (founded 1797), in 1903 (top), and in 1975 (bottom).

of September."[17]   Why September 8th? Very likely because that day was "the feast of the Nativity of Most Holy Mary," as he pointed out in one of his periodic reports to Governor Borica.

As always, Fr. Lasuén faced the problem of making the final choice of an exact location for this next mission. When in August, 1795, Fr. Vicente de Santa María had examined the region between Missions San Buenaventura and San Gabriel, his selection of a site had raised doubts in Fr. Lasuén's mind.[18]   It was only 8 or 9 leagues from San Gabriel and as many as 16 or 17 from San Buenaventura. Besides, it was more than 2 leagues away from El Camino Real, and therefore rather too isolated. The matter seemed to Fr. Lasuén at that time to require further discussion, and perhaps exploration. But in September, 1797, he accepted Fr. Vicente's choice without voicing doubts or making fresh surveys of his own. Probably by this time he was too weary and too rushed for time to want any delays. So on September 8 he founded Mission San Fernando in its present location, in a valley which Fr. Crespi's diary entry on August 5, 1769, had titled after Santa Catalina de Bononia de los Encinos (Catherine of Bologna, a Franciscan tertiary who died in 1463).[19]

The patron saint of Mission San Fernando Rey de España was the same saint after whom Fr. Lasuén's College of San Fernando in Mexico City was named. Ferdinand III of Castile (1199-1252), a Spanish hero-king, united the kingdoms of Castile and León, drove the Moors from Andalusia, and founded the University of Salamanca. The act which specially endeared him to Franciscans was his request to be buried in the Franciscan habit. Since this privilege was commonly granted at the time of his death to members of the Third Order of St. Francis, he has always been regarded as having been a Franciscan tertiary during his lifetime.

Notes

1. On the feast of St. Joseph, March 19, 1794, however, Fr. Lasuén blessed and dedicated "the very beautiful church of this mission (Santa Barbara) and there was all the solemnity, splendor, peace, and joy one could desire. Thanks be to God." Kenneally, *Lasuen* I, 302.

2. Kenneally I, 363.

3. Kenneally I, 368-69.

4. Engelhardt, *Missions and Missionaries* II, 493-94.

5. Engelhardt II, 494.

6. Kenneally II, 25-26.

7. Kenneally II, 26-28.

8. Kenneally I, 369.

9. Engelhardt II, 492, 494; Kenneally II, 30: ". . . in a beautiful place called Oroyjon by the natives, some of whom were present and showed themselves well pleased."

10. Kenneally I, 369.

11. Kenneally II, 31-32.

12. Engelhardt II, 491, 495.

13. Kenneally I, 368.

14. Kenneally II, 37.

15. Kenneally II, 38.

16. Kenneally II, 40.

17. Kenneally II, 42-44.

18. Kenneally I, 368.

19. Engelhardt II, 495; Bolton, *Historical Memoirs* II, 138; Kenneally II, 44: ". . . in a beautiful region known as Achois Comihabit by the natives, and located between the missions of San Buenaventura and San Gabriel."

8/Mission San Luis Rey (1798)
Fr. Lasuén's Last Years (1798-1803)

After founding Mission San Fernando on September 8, Fr. Lasuén might seem to have had plenty of time left before the end of the year in which to set up his fifth and last mission, under the patronage of San Luis Rey de Francia. But the obstacle did not consist in calendar time. It lay partly in the problem of location. Upon looking over the territory between Mission San Diego and Mission San Juan Capistrano in one of the 1795 expeditions, Fr. Mariner had proposed a site at Pala, which Fr. Lasuén had visited personally and had judged quite unsuitable for a mission.[1] Besides having other drawbacks it was much too far inland, nearly 20 miles from El Camino Real, and likewise too distant from the main centers of Indian population, which hugged the coastline and which most sorely needed Christian instruction. Fr. Lasuén could not avoid the conclusion that he must make a search of his own for a better place.[2] The problem of location was complicated by the impossibility of finding anywhere in California the priests to staff the new mission. They simply were not available in the autumn of 1797. Fr. Lasuén would have to wait for the eight new missionaries expected to arrive next year.

He was not one, however, to waste the autumn in idle

105

waiting. By September 23 he had moved south to Mission San Juan Capistrano, where he gathered all the freight intended for Mission San Luis Rey de Francia "so that I may be in a position to proceed as soon as possible" with the founding of that mission. He used San Juan Capistrano as a base from which to scan the area between it and San Diego. Guarded by Corporal Mario Verdugo and an escort of soldiers from the San Diego presidio, and accompanied by Fr. Juan Norberto, he revisited the Pala location between October 2 and 8, 1797, and confirmed his conviction that no mission should be built there.[3] In addition to its remoteness, he found that its soil was sparse and poor as well as too narrowly enclosed by surrounding hills. In after years Pala easily supported a small but famous *asistencia*, but it had not the resources to maintain a full-sized mission.

On the other hand, well situated on the coast about midway between San Diego and San Juan Capistrano, stretched the valley which Fr. Crespi in his diary entry for July 18, 1796, had praised as a potential site and had named after San Juan Capistrano. The founders of Mission San Juan Capistrano in 1776 had passed over this valley and had placed that mission a number of miles to the north. Since that time Fr. Crespi's valley had become known as "El Viejo"—the old San Juan Capistrano valley.[4] Nevertheless when Fr. Lasuen inspected it now, in 1797, he was impressed by it as offering the best situation for Mission San Luis Rey in that part of the country where he was expected to found it. He was not blind to its physical deficiencies, especially the lack of timber and firewood. But it enjoyed an excellent water supply and it had the supreme virtue of being already inhabited by a large population of Indians friendly in disposition and virtually begging for religious conversion.[5]

By October 20 Fr. Lasuén was at San Diego, writing to

both Governor Borica and the Father Guardian of his College of San Fernando summarizing his findings and urging
outright that Mission San Luis Rey be placed in the old
San Juan Capistrano valley. Just to make sure, he promised
to examine another possible site in "another valley called
Las Flores." He did so, but rejected it. Returning to "El
Viejo" on November 8 to 9 he scouted it again: "In the best
part of it," he wrote to the Father Guardian, "I placed a
cross which I did not bless, just to mark the place. I observed no other ceremony beyond reciting the Litany of Mary
Most Holy, and a prayer in honor of St. Louis, King of
France."[6] This cross later served as the center of Mission
San Luis Rey, yet Fr. Lasuén clearly regarded what he had
done not as a founding of the mission but only as a preliminary step towards it. Having no missionaries to put in
charge, he simply left the cross standing there alone, and
went on to Mission San Buenaventura to spend the winter
months.

Fr. Lasuén seems to have developed for the planned San
Luis Rey Mission an emotional attachment he felt for no
other, perhaps because he particularly liked the Indians
living in and near "El Viejo." On November 28, 1797, he
actually proposed to Governor Borica that when the mission
could be founded, if more neophytes should come to live
there than it could properly sustain, some of them might
be allowed to live part-time in their home villages, as was
being done at Mission San Diego.[7] Yet this was exactly the
kind of breach of the Franciscan mission system which Fr.
Serra had fought so hard against Governor Neve to prevent,
and which remained a living issue all during the mission
period in California. Fortunately, Mission San Luis Rey
turned out to be quite capable of housing and supporting
all its neophytes; so the breach never actually occurred.

During the winter and spring of 1789 at Mission San

Buenaventura Fr. Lasuén's thoughts, it seems, seldom strayed far from the needs of San Luis Rey. At the end of February he was hoping to go in April or May to the site where he had placed the cross, in order to push forward preparations for the foundation and to see whether he could overcome the problem of the scarcity of wood for building. By mid-April he was asking Fr. Vicente Fuster to see whether by distributing food to the Indians of the region he could persuade them "to make four or five little huts like those of the Channel, leaving vacant the space around the cross which I put in place, and . . . do a little planting, even if it were no more than an almud of corn, in soil moist enough for the purpose."[8] An influenza epidemic which struck down Fr. Fuster and many of the Indians frustrated this scheme. Fr. Lasuén himself fell victim to it, and he went to Mission Santa Barbara to recover.

The landing of eight new missionaries at Santa Barbara on May 8, 1798, from the frigate *Concepción* found Fr. Lasuén all but waiting at the dock. Their meeting was postponed, however, by quarantine for a smallpox epidemic. These were the missionaries Fr. Lasuén had been expecting since the previous year. He lost no time in assigning the newcomers tentatively to seven missions, usually one to each to help the veteran priests already there. For the prospective Mission San Luis Rey he chose Fr. José Faura to accompany Fr. Peyri. With these two and with the mule train of supplies earmarked for the mission Fr. Lasuén departed in early June for the spot where he had elevated the cross in November.

On June 13, 1798, the feast day of San Antonio de Padua, Fr. Lasuén dedicated Mission San Luis Rey de Francia "in this place known as Tacayme by the natives and as San Juan Capistrano by our first discoverers, midway between the missions of San Juan Capistrano and San Diego" with the blessing of earth, water, and the cross, and the singing of

San Luís Rey de Francia Mission (founded 1798), in 1903 (top), and in 1975 (bottom).

high Mass.[9] Present were not only the other priests and the soldier garrison but also "many neophytes who had come from San Juan Capistrano and San Diego missions to do preliminary work here, and by a great multitude of pagans of both sexes and all ages." Within two hours the pagans offered for baptism 25 boys and 29 girls, whom Fr. Lasuén baptized forthwith. But 19 adults who wished to be baptized then and there he relegated to classes in Christian catechism.

The saint named as patron of the mission was Louis IX, king of France (1214-70), noted for his passion for equal justice tempered with mercy for poor and rich alike, for his personal purity of life, and for his two crusades (1248, 1270) against the Moslems, on the second of which he died. He showed favor to the growth of orders of friars, especially the Friars Minor, whom he established in Paris about the year 1240. He was canonized in 1297 and is honored as the patron of the Third Order of St. Francis, of which he was a member. The Spanish Franciscans in California revered him enough for Fr. Crespi to name a valley near Point Conception for him on August 24, 1769, on the first Portolá expedition. His feast is observed on August 25.

Why Viceroy Branciforte in 1796 should have included Louis IX of France as one of the five to become patrons of the new missions he authorized is anybody's guess. He may have merely picked the name out of Crespi's diary or one of its successors as that of a Franciscan saint. But it is natural to suspect a political motive. Branciforte, or his king in Madrid, may have used this way to express sympathy for Louis XVI, who had been guillotined in January, 1793. To religious men of royalist sympathies this guillotining made him a martyr to be equated with his saintly namesake of the thirteenth century.

Already off to a good start, Mission San Luis Rey flourished mightily. A week after its foundation the number of

the baptized had grown to 77, and of catechumens to 23.[10]
Many more desired instruction but, as Fr. Lasuén sadly
reported, there was not enough food yet for so many. For
lack of housing accommodations at the mission, evidently
large numbers of Indians still lived in their native villages.
Fr. Lasuén, however, went about speedily providing living
quarters for all who wished them. He had borrowed 15
working neophytes from Mission San Diego and as many
more from Mission San Juan Capistrano. Using twenty
yoke of oxen these neophytes gathered adobe for many
hundreds of bricks, built corrals for cattle and sheep, hauled
stone for building foundations and stored borrowed grain
in housing constructed for the padres and the soldiers. Fr.
Lasuén himself even went to San Diego to search personally
both the mission and the ships there for spare doors, win-
dows, tables, chairs, barrels, and other furniture and con-
tainers.

Fr. Lasuén maintained his special interest in Mission San
Luis Rey for months afterwards, and proudly itemized its
progress in letters to Governor Borica. A visit there on July
18, 1798, revealed 136 Indian children and adults baptized,
8 catechumens under instruction, 19 marriages performed,
more than 8000 adobe bricks made, 175 building frames
carpentered, five foundations of buildings laid, and so
forth.[11] Near the end of August Fr. Lasuén dropped in
again on his way to San Buenaventura and learned of still
other spectacular increases in all these categories. How much
easier this all was than the founding of missions in the
1770's, when at Mission San Luis Obispo, for example,
only 12 Indian children received baptism in the first 12
months. In the years between, the Indians had seen the advantages of belonging to a mission and were now eager to
be enrolled.

One of the factors which worried Fr. Lasuén in January,

1797, before he began founding the five new missions was Governor Borica's failure to promise that the troops assigned to guard them would be additional soldiers, not merely men withdrawn from the guards of missions already existing.[12] In the latter event the existing ones might lose many neophytes, since "the majority of our neophytes have not yet acquired much love for our way of life; and they see and meet their pagan relatives in the forest, fat and robust and enjoying complete liberty." This fear he confided to his college in a letter of January 21. By the end of November, 1798, he wrote that what he had feared was actually taking place: "The governor is reducing the size of the escorts of most of the missions in order to supply those newly founded."[13] Or, as he said in a letter of June 28, 1799: " . . . although the number of establishments was increased by five there was no increase in the number of troops."

This was an ominous development, and not only solely from the missionaries' standpoint. Conditions in Europe being what they were, the government in Mexico City kept all its soldiers at home and could not increase the California garrisons. Borica would have been happy to guard all missions heavily if he had the necessary troops, but since he did not, he spread the mission guards more thinly and kept his major forces concentrated in the four presidios. Consequently he made no more splurges in ordering the foundation of more missions. Similarly, the Franciscan college in Mexico City received fewer and fewer missionaries from Spain, and experienced difficulty in answering Fr. Lasuén's continuing pleas for more recruits. He had to inform the college on November 29, 1800, that because of four probable retirements in the following year he would need at least that many replacements. Fr. Lasuén went on to remind the Father Guardian how large the priestly burden had grown: "We have now reached the stage . . . in which forty missionaries are needed in these missions . . ."[14] Feeling the pinch, the college showed no eagerness to increase it by increasing the number of missions. Also the government continued to have difficulties in keeping up the usual flow of supplies to its distant province. All told, nobody felt any great urge at this time to expand the California missions. Consequently none was established after 1798 until Mission Santa Inés in September, 1804.

Between 1798 and his death in 1803 Fr. Lasuén had other problems to occupy his mind. Bishop Francisco Rouset of Sonora, for example, was making a determined bid to bring California into his diocese and to assert his jurisdiction in ecclesiastical affairs over the missionaries there. As early as April, 1797, Bishop Rouset had demanded from Fr. Lasuén a full description of all the California missions in general and of each one in particular. Annual and biennial reports of each mission had always been sent by the president of the missions to the governor, the viceroy and particularly to the College of San Fernando. This demand by the bishop looked to Fr. Lasuén like an attempt by the bishop to replace the college. Nevertheless Fr. Lasuén prepared and sent to him a detailed written *Report of the Establishments of New California*.[15]

Hearing in September, 1801, that the bishop was considering sending a visitor to inspect the missions, Fr. Lasuén wrote in great agitation to the college asking what he should do if a visitor came: "I have never seen, known, or heard of such a procedure in the case of missions among pagans, and consequently I am entirely ignorant as to how to act in such a case."[16] In November Bishop Rouset required from Fr. Lasuén the names and locations of all his missionaries, together with lists of supplies sent to the "settlements, *doctrinas,* parishes and chapels." By using this terminology the bishop was contending that the missions were not true missions but parishes and *doctrinas* (as Governor Neve had done twenty years before), and therefore subject to his ecclesiastical jurisdiction. Acting under advice from his college, Fr. Lasuén told the bishop that he yearly supplied all such information to the college and the governor. But he neither agreed nor refused to supply it to the bishop too. By such evasions the California missionaries remained free of any other church authority except that of their own college during the whole of the mission period.

For the reasons just outlined Fr. Lasuén founded no more missions during the remaining five years of his life. But he did bring another one close to foundation, the future Mission Santa Inés, though no name had yet been suggested for it. Early in 1798, even before Mission San Luis Rey had been dedicated, Governor Borica was weighing the need for a new mission some thirty miles northeast of Mission Santa Barbara and on the eastern side of the coastal hills in the district known to Indians as Calahuasa. Fr. Lasuén felt torn by the arguments pro and con. But on February 1, 1798, he wrote to his college advocating that if a mission were erected there it should be named "after Francis Solano, or some other saint of the Order"[17] — Franciscan, of course.

By October, 1798, Fr. Lasuén had made up his mind that he must have a first-hand report on the missionary possibilities of the region under consideration. So when in that month a military expedition under Captain Felipe de Goycoechea set out from the Santa Barbara presidio to survey the military value of having such a mission, Fr. Lasuén sent along Fr. Estevan Tapis to examine it from the missionary point of view. Fr. Tapis came back with the information that the country in question had 13 rancherias with a population of about 1100 Indians. These were in constant contact with the Tulares savages who "at the words of their wizards or medicine men" periodically raided the lowland missions.

Like a good missionary, Fr. Lasuén could not resist the challenge to Christianize and civilize all these pagan tribes.[18]

Accordingly, on November 30, 1798, Fr. Lasuén wrote again to Fr. Miguel Lull, the guardian of San Fernando college. As instructed, Fr. Lasuén had told the governor that the college had now so many missions that it could hardly supply friars for any more. But, he added, "this one foundation is the only one that is needed in order to bring within reach of the entire pagan population both civilization and their incorporation into holy Church, for it is situated in the very center of this conquest which extends from San Diego to San Francisco."[19] A glance at the map shows that he was right on the matter of the proposed mission's central location in the whole California mission chain.

On the basis of the expedition's report Governor Borica promptly wrote to Mexico recommending the new establishment for reasons both military and religious. The mills ground slowly there, but on March 2, 1803, Viceroy Iturrigaray ordered payment of the normal 1000 pesos to the college for expenses. He then gave the signal to the incumbent governor to go ahead, and the latter wrote the permission to Fr. Lasuén on April 29. But Fr. Lasuén had already gone to his long rest. His successor as president of the California missions was none other than Fr. Estevan Tapis, the same man who had made the survey five years before. Fr. Tapis advised, under the circumstances, an unusually strong guard of soldiers for Mission Santa Inés.

Notes

1. Kenneally, *Lasuén* I, 368.

2. Kenneally II, 45.

3. Kenneally II, 45, 50.

4. Kenneally II, 49-51.

5. Kenneally II, 50n.

6. Kenneally II, 59.

7. Kenneally II, 60.

8. Kenneally II, 78.

9. Kenneally II, 84.

10. Kenneally II, 86 ff.

11. Kenneally II, 90.

12. Kenneally II, 6.

13. Kenneally II, 103-04; 122.

14. Kenneally II, 173.

15. Kenneally II, 21-24.

16. Kenneally II, 245-53.

17. Kenneally II, 69.

18. Engelhardt, *Missions and Missionaries* II, 599-601.

19. Kenneally II, 102.

9/The Last Three Missions (1804-23)

Waiting for the feast day of Santa Inés (Agnes) to roll around on January 21 would have meant too long a delay. So on September 17, 1804, in the presence of a large contingent of soldiers from the Santa Barbara presidio and many Indians from the neighboring missions at Santa Barbara and Purísima Concepción, Fr. Tapis and several colleagues inaugurated the new establishment under St. Agnes' patronage. St. Agnes, virgin and martyr, who died in or about the year 204, was one of the most famous of Roman maidens executed for her faith. Her presence rounded out the company of virgin martyrs who gave their names to the Santa Barbara Channel and some of its islands, as well as some of the missions and the mountains on its shore. There can be little doubt that Mission Santa Inés would never have been built had its location not guarded the passes against raiding inland tribes. Yet when a revolt by its Indian converts broke out in 1824 not enough soldiers were present at the mission even to try to put down the rebellion. They had to come from Santa Barbara. Evidently a concentration of forces at Santa Barbara presidio was deemed sufficient to keep the peace at all the missions in its neighborhood.

Several times during the years after Mission Santa Inés had been founded it looked as if Fr. Tapis might be called upon to found additional missions still father inland. Tribes from the interior valleys behind the whole length of the mission ladder found it more and more profitable to steal livestock from the coastal establishments as their herds increased. The marauders then had only to retreat eastward across the mountain ranges to be safe from pursuit. Militarily, some information about their strength became imperative, and the possibilities of setting up missions among them looked attractive to the Franciscan padres.

In 1806, therefore, bodies of Spanish soldiery from all four of the chief presidios made concerted excursions into the central valleys, accompanied by friars who kept their eyes open for potential new mission sites.[1] Those ranging between the latitudes of Mission San Francisco and San Miguel noted only four or five acceptable sites. Others penetrating the hinterlands between San Diego and Monterey left no record of their findings, perhaps an eloquent enough sign that they discovered nothing that pleased them. An expedition of 1810 from San José probing the valley of the San Joaquin and Merced rivers fared no better. Not that water, fertile land and pagan Indians did not abound. But the explorers, both fighting men and friars, seem to have been oppressed by a realization of the vast numbers of soldiers, and priests who would be needed to man missions and presidios in the interior, as well as to maintain communications with the far-off establishments along the Pacific coast. No such quantities of soldiers, or missionaries either, were at all likely to come to Alta California in the near future. In fact, they never came. After the War of Independence broke out in Mexico in 1810, the governors of the province felt that they needed what little strength they could muster to protect their long coastline against the foreign ships increasingly plying Pacific waters. The vital strength which had pushed Spain as far north as San Francisco Bay was ebbing, and none remained for further expansion. Defeats both in

Santa Inés Mission (founded 1804), in 1903 (top), and in 1975 (bottom).

Europe and in the New World soon tore apart much of what she had already accomplished.

Without planning, almost by accident, two final missions yet remained to be founded in the second and third decades of the nineteenth century: San Rafael, Arcángel, on December 14, 1817, and San Francisco Solano on July 4, 1823.

Mission San Rafael was not a mission to begin with but an *asistencia* of Mission Dolores of San Francisco. The latter had so many sick converts who were not recovering in the chill and foggy climate of the Bay that the fathers there in desperation decided to build a hospital for them in the drier, sunnier climate some miles to the north across the Bay.[2] Fr. Prefect Sarría was reluctant to plant an *asistencia* of that kind among the many pagan rancherias there. He was prevailed upon to agree, however, when Fr. Luis Gil y Taboada, renowned among Franciscans for his knowledge of medicine, volunteered (under some pressure, to be sure) to take charge of it. To a quiet cove among the hills where the city of San Rafael now stands he transported in 1817 all the seriously ill converts from Mission Dolores. With some new converts from the local Indians he soon had a community of over 300. Under Fr. Gil's direction they built a single large plain building, 40 ft. by 90 ft., divided into separate quarters for a hospital, a chapel, a storeroom, and a *monjerio* to house the unmarried girls. Two years later Fr. Juan Amorós took the place of Fr. Gil and was so successful that by 1822 his charges numbered 1000. On October 19 of that year San Rafael was therefore raised to full mission rank.

As a sanatorium for the sick the *asistencia* at its founding on December 14, 1817, was fittingly put under the patronage of San Rafael, Arcángel, because by Catholic tradition the Archangel Raphael was a healer of physical disease. This tradition rested on his name, which was Hebrew for "God

San Rafael Arcángel Mission (founded 1817), in 1903 (top), and in 1975 (bottom).

heals;" and he was therefore thought to be the angel who stirred the health-giving pool in the Gospel of John 5:2-4. In the Biblical Book of Tobit (3:25; 5:5ff) Raphael also was the angel who restored the sight of Tobias and drove the demon out of unmarriageable Sara.[3] Being a medical healer himself Fr. Gil y Taboada certainly knew this tradition and seems most likely to have chosen Rafael as patron of the *asistencia*.

California's 21st and final mission was founded at Sonoma on July 4, 1823, under conditions of confusion and divided authority which testified to the break-down of the mission chain of command after Mexico had won its independence from Spain in 1822. Shortly after 1820 Fr. José Altimira, a young and new arrival in California, was assigned to Mission Dolores in San Francisco. Hemmed in on the north and south by two prospering missions, San Rafael and Santa Clara, the mission near the San Francisco presidio was moribund. Fr. Altimira, with the approval of Governor Arguello but against the strong opposition of his Franciscan superior, Fr. Prefect Señán, resolved to abandon Mission Dolores and to transfer its inhabitants and possessions to the north of San Rafael. Indeed, he had decided to incorporate Missions San Rafael and Dolores into one new one at Sonoma. This imperious idea naturally roused vehement resistance in Fr. Amorós of San Rafael. Nevertheless Fr. Altimira led a search party north and raised a cross July 4, 1823, on a site in Sonoma which he called "new Mission San Francisco." After a conference Fr. Prefect Señán permitted Fr. Altimira to proceed with his mission, but absolutely vetoed both the abondonment of Mission Dolores and any attempt to absorb Mission San Rafael.

Fr. Altimira had to be satisfied with taking from Dolores in early August 700 neophytes and some supplies, including livestock. Priests in other missions were not disposed to help

San Francisco Solano Mission (founded 1823), in 1903 (top), and in 1975 (bottom).

the brash young man. The Russians at Fort Ross, however, gave him bells and numerous other articles. With this aid he completed and dedicated a completely wooden church on April 4, 1824, and at this time first called his establishment Mission San Francisco Solano. But Fr. Altimira proved to be unable to persuade his neophytes not to desert the mission in large numbers in order to return to their rancherias. After two years he gave up in disgust and asked to be transferred south to Mission San Buenaventura, which he was permitted to do.[4]

San Francisco de Solano (1549–1610) deserved a better mission. A Franciscan friar sent from Spain in 1589 to do missionary work among the Indians of South America, he labored for twenty years in Argentina and Paraguay, making immense journeys through jungles, preaching, founding many missions, and in his last years exhorting to repentance the inhabitants of Lima and Trujillo, Peru, by his fiery sermons and predictions. His name had appeared before on the lips and in the writings of the Franciscans in California. On July 24, 1769, Fr. Crespi's diary called a handsome valley near the future Los Angeles "San Francisco Solano Apostle of America."[5] Fr. Danti in 1795 picked out a mission site on the east side of San Francisco Bay and give it the saint's name, only to have it altered by the viceroy to Mission San José in 1797. After many postponements the Apostle of America thus finally became patron of the last and short-est-lived of all the California missions. Eleven years after its foundation Mission San Francisco Solano succumbed to secularization in 1834, when Governor Vallejo seized its lands and properties for his own.

Notes

1. Engelhardt, *Missions and Missionaries* II, 623-24.

2. Chase and Saunders, *California Padres,* p. 387; *California's Missions* ed. Ralph B. Wright (Los Angeles: The Sterling Press, 1950), p. 89.

3. Butler, *Lives of the Saints* IV, 187; Attwater, *Penguin Dictionary of Saints,* p. 245.

4. *California's Missions,* p. 94.

5. Fr. Crespi's Diary in Bolton, *Historical Memoirs* II, 124-24: "Because we arrived at this place today, the day of San Francisco Solano, Apostle of America, we gave it his name, so that with his intercession the conversion of these docile heathen may be accomplished by founding for them on this spot a mission dedicated to him as patron, since the place and docility of the heathen invite it . . . ."

10/Overview

No one man, not even Fr. Serra, ever had the complete say in founding any California mission. In retrospect, such an enterprise involved questions of timing, location, naming, the availability of soldiers as well as missionaries to man the mission, the buying and transporting of supplies, and other considerations, which required the cooperation of religious, military, and civilian officials on many levels of the governing hierarchy.

The source of all authority began, of course, in Madrid, where the king and his Council for the Indies laid down general policy for all missionary activity in the New World. This policy normally rested on a written code of laws known as *Las Leyes de las Indias.* But the king could also act with naked power, as he did when in 1767 he ordered the viceroy to expel all Jesuits from the New World immediately. This action gave the Franciscans of the College of San Fernando their foothold in Baja California.

Other interventions by Madrid had less happy results in Franciscan eyes. Its creation of the Internal Provinces, as a separate unit embracing California, under Teodoro de Croix on August 22, 1776, interposed between Fr. Serra and the friendly Viceroy Bucareli a semimilitary government much less well disposed toward Franciscan mission methods and aims.[1] And in June 1782, the king's backing of Bishop Antonio de los Reyes of Sonora in a scheme of reorganizing the missions into local *custodies* under the bishop's own jurisdiction threatened to separate the missionaries from their religious superiors in Mexico City.[2] This scheme would certainly have wrecked the Franciscan mission system in California; but, after watching it in operation in one trial *custody* in Sonora, the king and his advisors withdrew the royal support. In 1801 Fr. Lasuén had to stave off a similar attempt by a later bishop of Sonora, Bishop Rouset, to treat the missions as parishes in order to bring them under his control.[3] In short, the California missionaries never knew when a thunderbolt from Madrid might not threaten the fruits of their labors.

As the king's personal representative the viceroy in Mexico City had supreme power over all civilian and military affairs throughout Mexico, even to its most distant provinces. He also had a degree of control over the Franciscan College of San Fernando.[4] The royal decree which licensed that college on October 15, 1733, stipulated that the college must hold itself ready to provide missionaries on demand by the viceroy. Fr. Serra could and often did write to the Father Guardian of the college asking for more missionaries whenever new missions were to be founded in California, but he always wrote also to the viceroy to request permission to found. The viceroy and the Fathers Guardian then usually conferred to determine how many priests could actually be spared by the college, which had other obligations to fulfill, and how many new missions the viceroy judged that he had the resources to establish at the time. These resources included every type of supplies for making the mission a self-supporting agricultural enterprise, as well as the ships to transport them to California by sea or the mules to carry them by land, assuming that the overland route opened by Anza in 1774 and 1776 was not being blocked at the time by hostile Yuma Indians. The viceroy also had to plan how to get enough soldiers to California to allow each mission the customary guard of at least six, and to keep the presidios strongly garrisoned. If either the college or the viceroy could not provide what was needed at the time, any proposed new mission was temporarily postponed. But not for long. A number of times the college sent an emissary to Spain to recruit more members to serve as missionaries.[5] And the viceroy would somehow contrive to find the requisites he was asked to supply. Until civil war broke out in Mexico in 1810, viceroy and college cooperated without any serious friction in the push to move the Spanish presence northward up the California coast.

The viceroy also had the right to name the patron saint of each new mission and to choose the general area of its location. As to the naming, the practice had long been established by Gálvez as visitador that the missions of the Franciscans in California should be dedicated to saints of the Franciscan Order. Not being a Franciscan himself, the viceroy might not know who the most appropriate saints were. In that case he had only to consult the college or get hold of a Franciscan *Ordo* or calendar or, for that matter, read a journal by Fr. Crespi or Fr. Font. The problem of indicating the proper site for a mission usually offered more difficulty. The viceroy had never seen California or founded a mission, but he could read the priests' diaries or the printed accounts by Fages and Costansó, or receive oral reports from returned explorers like Anza. And, of course, he had long and detailed letters from Fr. Serra or Fr. Lasuén and their successors, as well as annual and biennial reports for each mission already in existence. Nor were the friars his only correspondents. Frequent reports reached him from the governor giving information, not always consistent with what he received from the friars but at least in agreement about the geography of California. All these data enabled him to point to the general area where the mission should go. Inspection of specific sites, and choice of them, the viceroy left to the priests and soldiers on the ground in California.

Such conflicts as might occur in Mexico City between a viceroy's conception of a mission and that held by the College of San Fernando remained largely theoretical and impersonal. On the local level at Monterey, however, they tended to sharpen into clashes between the governor and the president of the missions on highly specific issues, sometimes embittered by personal feelings. Captain Fages and Fr. Serra parted company on the question whether the soldiers guarding a mission or the padres teaching Christianity there should adjudicate and punish offenses by the resident Indians. Viceroy Bucareli might write letters to Governor Rivera urging the founding of certain missions requested by Fr. Serra, but on more than one occasion Rivera would refuse on the ground that the military risks were too great at that time. Neve had orders to found Channel missions, specifically one at Santa Barbara, but tried to avoid going ahead with them because he disapproved of Franciscan mission methods.

In the confirmation controversy with Fr. Serra one might wonder at Neve's interference in religious affairs, but it was the result of the *real patronato* (royal patronage) exercised by the Spanish king to approve or to veto any appointments made by the pope to ecclesiastical offices anywhere in Spanish America, and to do the same with any extraordinary powers conferred by the pope on Spanish missionaries. Neve claimed that the king had conferred on him the right to exercise the *real patronato* over the California missions, which gave him the ability to control the missions in numerous indistinct ways, and specifically to stop Fr. Serra from using the faculty of administering the sacrament of confirmation unless the king and the viceroy had approved it by a formal written *pase.* Tracing the ramification of the impact of this *real patronato* on religious affairs at many levels of government would require a separate book. Suffice it to say that the very existence of the *real patronato* hung like a cloud over the missions whenever California had a governor like Neve who claimed the right to use it. Fortunately, that right was seldom invoked.

Providentially the money for the mission enterprise in California never had to come out of the viceroy's budget. He drew it all from the Pious Fund raised in 1697 by the Jesuits, Frs. Salvatierra and Ugarte, for their mission expenses in Baja California.[6] They collected from devout residents of Mexico City 43,000 pesos, the unexpended portion of which was invested in land ventures in Mexico. When the Jesuits were expelled in 1767, the Fund became a special branch of the *real hacienda* (royal treasury) administered by a director-general named Mangino under the supervision of the viceroy.[7] By April, 1793, Viceroy Revilla Gigedo estimated the Fund's total value at the staggering sum of 715,500 pesos, which he calculated *should* yield an annual income of 35,575 pesos, much more than the 22,000 pesos per year required for the support of the California missions then existing.[8] But no such income was being produced because the estates making up the Fund were being allowed to go to ruin. Therefore, Rivella Gigedo argued, the Spanish expansion northward should stop, for purely financial reasons.

So large a sum restricted to missionary use had been a temptation since 1767 to those who longed to spend it for less religious purposes. The Real Tribunal de Cuentas had tried to protect the Fund by ruling on July 27, 1773, that "the said pious fund of California . . . ought to be employed only in payment of allowances (*sínodos*) to missionaries, troops, and ships of the same Peninsula, and for the establishment of the missions of San Diego and Monterey, and not diverted to other objects . . . ."[9] The then Viceroy Bucareli used it very effectively to develop the departure port of San Blas, to build and repair ships for the California run, and to finance the Anza expeditions of 1774 and 1776 opening up an overland trail to the pioneer province.[10] In addition Bucareli proposed that the Fund give each mission 800 pesos per year. Asked for his opinion, the royal treasurer replied that the Fund should pay more than the 10,000 pesos it was contributing annually. Whereupon the Fund's director, Mangino, replied that in fact it was paying out 14,879 pesos in 1773 for the California missions, besides 6139 pesos for transporting Dominicans from Vera Cruz to San Blas.[11]

Before long the Fund's gifts became standardized at 1000 pesos to each California mission to buy basic equipment at the time of its foundation, and a 400 peso stipend to each missionary for the purchase of church goods. Since Franciscan friars took a vow of poverty, and therefore could not regard any part of their stipends as personal property, the stipends did not constitute a form of salary. Considering all these uses for the Pious Fund, could the California missions have ever come into being without it?

The answer to that question probably is Yes, though with greater difficulty. The money would have been found somewhere. Spanish alarm over possible Russian and British efforts to move south from their settlements in Alaska and on the Columbia River during the latter part of the mission period reached clear back to Madrid and haunted the dreams of the viceroy and his advisers in Mexico City. (By regular voyages from Monterey, California, or San Blas, Mexico, as far north as the Gulf of Alaska, Spain claimed and controlled the entire Pacific coast of North America from 1774 to 1794.)

Gálvez, the king's visitador and a member of his Council of the Indies, was an ardent expansionist who gave his immense power and prestige to the conquest of California. In 1768–69 Spain had a group of extraordinary men to plan and execute the California enterprise. Besides Gálvez, she had viceroy Carlos de Croix, the soldier Portolá and, of course, Fr. Serra backed by the veteran Franciscans of the Sierra Gorda missions, many of them his personal friends. Viceroy Antonio Bucareli, the successor of De Croix in 1771, carried on the original impetus with great intelligence and sympathy until his death in 1779. Anza's expeditions showed abilities close to genius. Fr. Lasuén, carefully trained by Fr. Serra, stood ready to take over the presidency of the missions in 1784 when Fr. Serra died. Such men gave the settlement and conversion of Alta California a most auspicious start. It is hard to imagine that they would have allowed themselves to be stopped by finances if the Pious Fund had never existed.

The triumph of the Mexican Revolution in 1822 inevitably severed the ties between Mexico City and Madrid. It also did away with the Spanish viceroys, substituting for them a Mexican legislature. The governors of California, too, ceased to be aristocratic Spaniards with education and military or administrative experience basically sympathetic to the missions as essential to both Church and State, and became a less homogeneous group, many of them intent on enriching themselves. The College of San Fernando as a Spanish institution fell under suspicion. In short, the whole chain of command which had regulated and sustained the California missions lay shattered.

This chaos was of a sort fitted to produce a missionary like Fr. Altimira, whose egocentric ambitions made him careless alike of his religious superiors and the rights of his brother missionaries in founding Mission San Francisco de

Solano in 1823. Problems with his Indian converts led to his desertion from the mission within two years. A decade later he fled California secretly by ship, a sad contrast with the founders of the California missions some sixty-five years before. And a prophetic prologue to the coming death of the mission system under the scramble for their lands and possessions by Mexican grantees which followed hard upon the passage of the secularization law in 1834. From that law the California mission system never recovered. Under American rule and after the Civil War the mission churches were indeed reborn; but by one of the ironies of history, they lived on only as parish churches after all.

In recent years, however, they have begun to assume a wider role. Restored from ruin and increasingly proud of their past, the twenty-one California missions have become centers of pilgrimage not only for the millions who live in the State but also for the many hundreds of thousands of travelers who drive through it every year. Some drawn by a hunger for religion, others by a search for historical roots, still others by the beauty and strangeness of mission architecture, by curiosity, by custom, by unknown promptings of the heart, visitors pour in by car and bus. They hear Masses or wander about the gardens or explore the historical museum in which each mission displays the relics of its early years. Under other forms, the "Old Missions" of California still live on.

Notes

1. Geiger, *Serra* II, 152 ff.

2. Geiger II, 343-65.

3. Kenneally, *Lasuen* II, 245-53.

4. Geiger I, 91-96.

5. E. g., Fr. Rafael Verger's trip to Spain in 1767, Geiger I, 183.

6. Charles E. Chapman, *The Founding of Spanish California 1687-1783* (New York: Macmillan, 1916), p. 17; Alberta J. Dennis, *Spanish Alta California* (New York: Macmillan, 1927), pp. 122-23; Herbert E. Bolton, *The Rim of Christendom* (New York: Russell and Russell, 1960), pp. 343, 581.

7. Denis, pp. 128, 260-61.

8. Chapman, p. 423.

9. Chapman, p. 128.

10. Denis, pp. 219, 325, 415.

11. Chapman, pp. 260-61.

Appendix I
The Development of the Missions of California

Since this book tells the story only of the founding of the old missions of California, it will be well to offer at least a brief summary of the subsequent history of each down to the present day.

Tourists who visit the old missions and see the impressive stone structures or massive adobe buildings at some of them sometimes think that their construction was begun when the missions were founded. The fact is that the beginnings were hard and the progress was as a rule slow. The first mission buildings were but rude shelters, poor huts of stakes roofed with tules. Then, ordinarily, better but comparatively small buildings of adobe with thatched roofs were put up; and only after a mission had developed sufficiently were the large and solidly built mission compounds constructed.

San Diego

When Fr. Serra founded Mission San Diego on July 16, 1769, he had to do so inside the confines of the Spanish camp, which contained not only priests but soldiers, sailors, and civilians, many of them ill. In that wild and unknown countryside, inhabited by Indians whose behavior was unforeseeable, there was no other practicable site where Fr. Serra could establish the mission at that time. It soon became clear, however, that the founding there had severe drawbacks. Frightened and angered by Portolá's expedition, the Indians did not come forward to receive baptism and conversion but only to steal what they could and, on at least one occasion, to attack the camp, from which they were repelled by musket fire.

Relations between the Franciscan friars and their potential converts had evidently got off on the wrong foot. In 1773 Fr. Palóu tried to remedy the breach by moving the mission some six miles inland, up the San Diego River, but the Indians had so thoroughly identified it with the hated camp that on November 4, 1775, they stormed the mission, killing a blacksmith, a carpenter, and a priest (Fr. Jayme).

The mission was then withdrawn back to the camp, and did not return to its inland site until July, 1776, when Fr. Serra himself took it there. By October a rough temporary church had been set up without opposition by the Indians, who by this time had learned the difference between a mission and a presidio. Neophytes arrived then in increasing numbers until Mission San Diego began to prosper both spiritually and materially. A large permanent church was completed on November 12, 1813. At its greatest prosperity the mission possessed some 50,000 acres on which grazed 20,000 sheep, 10,000 cattle, and over 1,000 horses.

But already by 1824 the lands of Mission San Diego were being nibbled away by a growing population of civilian settlers. The secularization laws of the 1830's expropriated all its possessions. And in 1846 the mission itself was virtually given away to Santiago Arguello, one of the inevitable harpies of secularization. He was not to enjoy it permanently, however. In 1862, Congress returned some 22 acres to the mission, which then resumed its spiritual functions.

When physical restoration of its buildings began in 1931, only some parts of the church were intact. These were incorporated into a new structure built in strict duplication of the original. Recently a long portico has been added. In 1975 the mission church was raised to the rank of a minor basilica.

San Carlos Borromeo

In earliest mission days all roads led to Monterey. There the governors of Alta California had their permanent residence, and there also the presidents of the California missions had their head-quarters at Mission San Carlos Borromeo, founded on June 3, 1770. At first, then, Monterey was like San Diego half presidio, half mission. But Fr. Serra, first of the presidents, having himself lived at San Diego from 1769-1770 in a similar situation, well knew that the Indians of the surrounding countryside would not come to a mission inside an armed presidio. The mission must be moved speedily to a location some distance away. So, early in 1771, he transferred it some five miles south to the mouth of the Carmel River.

There it grew slowly, the Indians still distrusting its connections with Monterey, as evidenced by the mission priests who rode into Monterey every Sunday to say Mass in the presidio church. Ships bringing food and supplies from Mexico were few and far between. And since the mission at first had too few neophytes working in the fields along the Carmel River its crops were often too scanty to feed both the mission and the garrison at Monterey, as was expected. Consequently both establishments lived constantly on the edge of hunger. Not until 1783 did the mission have even as many as 165 Indian converts.

Fr. Fermín Lasuén, succeeding Fr. Serra as president at the latter's death in 1784, likewise chose to live most of the time at Mission San Carlos. Nearness to the governor, the main channel of instructions and news from the viceroy in Mexico City, had obvious advantages. By 1797 Fr. Lasuén had built an impressive stone and adobe church for the mission. But until he died in 1803 he had to resist increasing pressure by civilian settlers from Mexico for surrender to them of slices of San Carlos' rich lands. These pressures were to culminate in the secularization decrees of 1833 which completely stripped the mission of its fields and even of its buildings. By 1836 the mission, abandoned by its priests, lay crumbling.

Only after it had been returned to the Roman Catholic Church by the United States government were the first efforts launched, in 1882, at least to preserve those ruins which still existed. Part of the church structure underwent restoration after 1924, and in 1933 it was solid and whole enough to become a parish church. Since then a whole series of restorations have been made, chiefly by Fr. Michael O'Connell, pastor after 1933, and by Harry Downie, an authority on mission architecture. By 1924 construction of the Serra Chapel in the mission gardens had been finished.

More recently, the church of Carmel Mission became a minor basilica when, in 1967, the diocese of Monterey-Fresno was divided and Monterey became a separate diocese under Bishop Henry Clinch.

San Antonio de Padua

Three years after its dedication by Fr. Serra on July 14, 1771, Mission San Antonio was doing so well that it had, besides 178 Indian neophytes, 68 cattle and seven horses, a promising harvest of corn and wheat, and a number of new buildings. And in order to facilitate religious instruction, Fr. Buenaventura Sitjar had translated the language of his neophytes into Spanish, a hard but useful labor.

In 1776 the crude adobe church was roofed with mortar and tiles, this being the first time (that we know of) when tiles were made to protect the roof of any California mission. The enlightened and energetic padres at Mission San Antonio in the same year built a whole street lined with adobe houses for their neophytes, as well as storerooms, barracks, warehouses, and shops. To top all, irrigation ditches were dug to carry water to the fields from the San Antonio River.

Building of one sort or another never stopped. In 1779-1780 a long building (133 feet) was erected for a church and sacristy. Later, a water mill for grinding grain. Then, as the Indian population steadily grew, it required wells, a reservoir, and an acqueduct. In 1813 a strong new church stood complete. Because of heavy rains in 1825 many structures collapsed, but they were soon replaced by larger and sturdier ones.

By 1830 the mission had over 8,000 cattle and 12,000 sheep. Its crops were large; wine making and basketry flourished. But secularization ruined Mission San Antonio in 1834. Revival began in 1862, when President Lincoln gave it back to the Roman Catholic Church. However, in 1882 the last priest living there died, and the mission long remained empty. Efforts at restoration began in 1903, but the great earthquake which almost flattened the city of San Francisco in 1906 undid the restoration at the mission also . The front of the church and a few arches alone survived.

The William Randolph Hearst Foundation in 1948 gave $50,-

000 to Mission San Antonio for its restoration. The restorers have tried so hard to be faithful to the methods of its original builders that they have actually used the same types of mission tools to cut and prepare every piece of timber in the same way as did the original workmen. Nature has cooperated by keeping the surroundings of oaks and of valley much as they were when the mission was established.

San Gabriel Arcángel

This mission, founded by Fr. Angel Somera and Fr. Benito Cambón on September 8, 1771, as instructed by Fr. Serra, lay in a wilderness penetrated before only by Portolá and his men. To Mission San Gabriel's south stood San Diego, merely a few days' journey, but to its north many hundreds of miles separated it from Monterey. And the crowds of Indians who surrounded the new mission, perhaps no more than curious at first, became so angered by the soldier guard that they launched an outright attack, as happened several times at San Diego.

Who would have dreamed that Mission San Gabriel, apparently so remote, would become in 1774 and 1776 De Anza's first point of contact with California? Or that in 1781 Rivera would make it the rendezvous for the two wings of his expedition? Or that in 1782 it would serve as a base for the settlers who founded the pueblo of Nuestra Señora Reina de los Angeles a few miles away?

Before Mission San Gabriel could become any of these things, however, it had first to become a going establishment. It did so, in the well proven manner, by pacifying and then converting to Christianity large numbers of Indians, by sowing crops and building buildings, and finally by starting a large permanent church in 1796. After the earthquake of 1812 had felled its bell tower, a beautiful new bell wall took its place.

As the pueblo of Los Angeles grew, its inhabitants began slowly moving onto whatever mission lands took their fancy. Secularization in 1834 then led to the usual mad scramble by settlers for these lands. The mission Indians, to whom these acres belonged, were often all too willing to part with them, and their cattle too, for whisky or gold. San Gabriel's 16,500 cattle dwindled to less than 100 in six years. By 1843 everything movable had been removed from the mission. And a sale of all its buildings by Governor Pio Pico was averted only by the coming of United States troops. In 1862, however, Congress returned to the Church all the mission buildings and a part of the adjacent land.

Today Mission San Gabriel is occupied by the Claretian Fathers, who keep the church in good condition and use it daily for Mass.

San Luis Obispo

The year 1771 being a year of hunger for the presidio at Monterey and for the two missions nearest it, Captain Pedro Fages in that year took a dozen of his men southward with him to hunt bears in Los Osos valley, where they abounded. He got his bears but, equally important, he won the friendship of the Chumash Indians living in that region. Without their help Fr. José Cavaller and the little band of men whom Fr. Serra left at Mission San Luis Obispo after founding it on September 1, 1772, could not have survived the winter.

What rescued the mission from complete dependence on Chumash generosity was the coming of Fr. Francisco Palóu in October, 1773, with nine Baja California Indian men, some of them with their families, to work the mission fields. He brought with him also plowshares and other essential agricultural equipment, carpenter tools, 41 cattle, and a few pigs, and numbers of horses and mules. With him came Fr. Juan Prestamero and Fr. José Murguía, the latter a sturdy veteran of the Sierra Gorda missions.

By the year 1800, for example, the mission was progressing very well indeed. It had 724 Indian converts; over 5,000 cattle, 6,000 sheep, 928 horses, and 80 mules. Crops of wheat, corn, beans, and peas were consistently large. Moreover, about 1793, it had completed the big mission church which still stands.

Secularization in August, 1834, set up over the mission a series of civil administrators, some of them honest. Grantees and squatters gobbled up its lands. But Fr. Ramón Abella hung on to possession of the church until his death in 1842 at the age of 72. Governor Pio Pico sold the entire mission, including its church, to the canny Yankee sea-captain John Wilson for $500 in 1845.

Happily this transaction was voided by the raising of the United States flag at Monterey on July 7, 1846. In 1851 President Buchanan, pursuant to an Act of Congress, granted back to the Roman Catholic Church all the mission buildings and a large tract of land covering much of what is now the business district of the city of San Luis Obispo. Most of this the Church has sold off to townspeople.

For many years during the latter part of the nineteenth century and the start of the twentieth the mission church and its auxiliary buildings were sheathed in wooden boards. Its three large bells hung in a Victorian steeple on the roof. This architectural ugliness did not deter the church, however, from adding an annex to its east in 1893, which gave it a stubby L-shape. This annex was later extended to become almost as long as the aisle of the main church.

In 1933 Fr. John Harnett began the task of stripping off the clapboard sheathing, pulling down the belfry, and rebuilding the bell wall in the front of the church. What was once an adobe Spanish mission has been serving for well over a century as a parish church in the diocese of Monterey (since 1967). One of its most precious possessions is a first class relic of the saint whose name the mission bears. It was obtained by Bishop Harry Anselm Clinch in Rome while attending the Second Vatican Council.

San Francisco de Asís, or Dolores

Fr. Serra would dearly have loved to establish this mission in honor of the great saint who founded his Order, but he was busy with the southern missions in 1776 when the time became ripe for doing so. As his deputies he sent Fr. Palóu and Fr. Cambón, who chose a site on La Laguna de Nuestra Señora de los Dolores (Our Lady of Sorrows). After waiting in vain for Governor Rivera to come for the official founding ceremonies, the two priests formally dedicated Mission San Francisco de Asís (Assisi) on October 8, 1776. St. Francis has had to give way to our Lady, however, and his mission is now known simply as Dolores.

Under whatever name, the mission never really caught hold. Its climate was too foggy and cold to encourage the growing of crops; the presidio set up by Lt. Moraga, at a spot first designated by his superior, Captain de Anza, a short distance away was too close; and escape eastward to the Berkeley side of the Bay was too easy. Moreover, epidemics of various diseases, trivial to the Spanish settlers but often fatal to the Indian converts, kept sweeping the mission. A church begun in 1782 was not finished until 1791. And the founding of Mission San Rafael in 1817 in the sunny lands north of the Bay of course drained away many of the remaining neophytes, including all who were sick.

Secularization in 1834 swept the mission lands into hands which were neither Indian nor Franciscan. Soon only the church and its auxiliary buildings remained. After the Civil War these structures were returned to the Catholic Church by the United States Congress, as at other missions. By that time the growing city population was already hemming in Mission Dolores.

Oddly enough, the earthquake of 1906, which destroyed so much of the city of San Francisco, inflicted no wounds at all on the mission church, either inside or outside. Its lovely redwood ceiling and its many statues, some created by Indian artists, remain intact today.

The church is now a museum, much visited. The large modern church of St. Francis next to it is a minor basilica and is called Mission Dolores Basilica.

San Juan Capistrano

After the official founding of this mission by Fr. Serra on November 1, 1776, an adobe church was constructed in 1777 and enlarged between 1783 and 1785. This served well the needs of Mission San Juan Capistrano until 1797. Then the same thing happened as was later to happen at Mission San Juan Bautista. Growing too optimistic about the numbers of Indians they expected to convert, the padres decided that they should build an immense new church. And this was to be made exclusively of stone, not mere adobe. For that purpose they commissioned an expert stone mason, Isidor Aguilar, to plan and construct the church. He designed not the flat ceiling of other missions but a more impressive one consisting of six large domes.

For years all labored, dragging up stones from the river beds and gullies to the site of the church. Aguilar died after six years, but they labored on as best they could, even adding a seventh dome as the structure seemed to require. By 1806 they had finished the long work proudly. And in 1812 the earthquake not only destroyed it utterly, but killed forty of the neophytes who happened to be inside the church at the time. A grievous blow to the other neophytes still under instruction.

The discouraged padres in charge did not even try to build the stone church again, but went back to using the adobe church of 1785. They turned their energies instead to constructing soap vats, brick kilns, tannery tanks and presses, and the like.

In 1818 the Argentine rebel Bouchard with two heavily gunned ships, after making the Monterey garrison retreat into the interior, out of range of his cannon, touched also at Mission San Juan Capistrano. His object was to rouse the Alta California Indians to rebellion. But Fr. Gerónimo Boscano, hearing of his coming, had fled into the back country with all his neophytes. Finding no Indians to lead in revolt, Bouchard's crews attacked only the mission's wine casks.

Mexico, having won its independence from Spain in 1822, sent to California governors who would free the Indians there from the same Spanish yoke. Governor Echeandia in 1824 told them that they were not bound to obey the Franciscans, and Governor Figueroa in 1833 designated Mission San Juan Capistrano a pueblo of free Indians. He died, however, before he could devise legal protection for their share in the mission properties. Accordingly, when secularization came its lands were taken over by Mexican settlers. Last scene of all to end the tragedy, Governor Pio Pico sold all its remaing properties to his brother-in-law and partner.

In 1865 the United States government returned part of the mission's lands to the Roman Catholic Church. But serious attempts to restore the buildings did not come until 1895, when the Landmarks Club started them. They were continued in 1910 by Fr. John O'Sullivan, who worked at the restoration for many years. In 1922 he discovered that rooms then in use as a granary and storeroom actually were the 1785 church.

This has become known as the Serra Chapel because it is the only church building standing today in which Fr. Serra is known to have celebrated Mass and administered baptism and confirmation. Fr. O'Sullivan renewed it, so that it is still serving today as the mission church. He never tried to rebuild the stone church, of which only a stretch of wall, a single dome, and a bell wall still exist.

Santa Clara de Asís

Situated some forty miles south of its twin in San Francisco, Mission Santa Clara de Asís was founded on January 12, 1777, by Lt. Moraga and Fr. Tomás de la Peña on the banks of the river named earlier by De Anza El Río de Nuestra Señora de Guadalupe. Blessed with a warm, bright climate and fertile, well watered lands, the mission faced none of the problems of sickness, poor farming, and the nearness of a distracting presidio which crippled the San Francisco Mission. As things turned out, however, it had to face different troubles of its own.

In the very year of the mission's founding Lt. Moraga led a band of De Anza's settlers to form the pueblo of San José just across the Río only a short distance away. Predictably, the attractions of this pueblo handicapped sorely the mission priests in their efforts first to baptize and then to hold the Indians who came to them for instruction in the Faith.

Moreover, the Río turned out to be an unreliable stream. It tended to flood the low-lying meadows around it. To escape these inundations the mission in 1784 had to abandon all the buildings at its first location, including a fine new church dedicated in that year by Fr. Serra, and to rebuild everything on higher ground. There, however, an earthquake ruined it in 1818. Again the padres grimly chose a third site some miles away and again rebuilt.

This time they had chosen well. They finished yet another church in 1822, and other necessary buildings by 1825. This church lasted until fire consumed it utterly in 1926. The present church at the University of Santa Clara is a replica of it.

All these changes of site and rebuilding of structures took a great deal of time and energy, but they did not curtail the mission's outdoor work in agriculture or its training of the women neophytes in such industries as weaving. In fact, on the whole, it did extremely well as a mission. But of course it lost all its lands and most of its buildings in the secularization debacle.

When the mission church and a fraction of the lands were returned to the Roman Catholic Church, the Jesuits took them over, in 1851, as a school. With their characteristic energy they advanced it to a college in 1855. Under their administration it is esteemed as a university today.

The only reminders of mission days now at Santa Clara are the cloister garden wall and a piece of the cross used in the first dedication ceremony of the mission in 1777.

San Buenaventura

Taking advantage of Governor Neve's absence, Fr. Serra founded Mission San Buenaventura on Easter Sunday, March 31, 1782, and set it going on the Franciscan model. This required, normally, two priests to be resident at every mission. Also, all neophytes were expected to leave their home rancherias and to live at the mission, where they could receive training, chiefly in religious matters but also in practical skills like agriculture, blacksmithing, carpentry, weaving, and the care of horses, mules, cattle, and other livestock.

Governor Neve, however, strongly favored the Arizona style of mission, which had been also the Jesuit style in Baja California. In this system each mission had only one priest, and his converts stayed in their home villages, where he visited them from time to time for religious instruction only. They learned none of the practical skills being taught in the Franciscan missions.

Mission San Buenaventura grew quickly. By 1809 it had built a large church of stone and masonry, not to mention an aqueduct system seven miles long feeding into a reservoir from which the fields received their water for irrigation. The soil produced a great variety of foods, especially grain. The mission was lucky enough to have a series of fine priests, including Fr. José Señán, later to become president of the California Missions.

When the 1812 earthquake wrecked the church's stone face, the padres pressed the work of reconstruction so that it took only three years. During a visit from the Argentine pirate Bouchard in 1818, the mission priests simply took their Indian neophytes inland, out of reach of his revolutionary talk as well as his ships' guns. Another crisis erupted in the next year when 22 Mojave Indians tried to stir up dissatisfaction among the mission's neophytes. In the end the mission soldiers drove away the intruders, killing ten of them and losing two of their own number.

Secularization in June, 1836, knelled the death of Mission San Buenaventura. Its first civil administrator, Rafael Gonzales, was both honest and efficient, but he could not stem the tide. By

1845 the mission's lands had all been broken up and sold.

The church building itself and a fraction of its former possessions were returned to the Catholic Church in 1862. The city of Ventura, having grown up around the mission church, now uses it for parish purposes.

Santa Barbara

Father Serra's founding of nine missions from 1769 to his death in 1784 is matched, in numbers at least, by the nine more founded by his successor, Father Lasuén, during the years of his tenure as president of the California missions from 1784 to 1803, the year of his death. All these foundations Fr. Lasuén attended personally. He was more fortunate than Fr. Serra in being hale of body and in having at Monterey a series of friendly governors. He benefited also by the advent, between 1790 and 1795, of stone.masons, carpenters, weavers, and other skilled craftsmen sent to Alta California by the authorities in Mexico City to teach their trades to the mission priests and neophytes. It was still necessary to begin missions with buildings of adobe and tule, but work could begin almost immediately on great stone churches with roofs of tile.

On the other hand, the later years of Fr. Lasuén's presidency were increasingly shadowed by the Napoleonic wars engulfing Europe. Whether because of Spain's need for help from her American colonies or because of her inability to export to them the kinds of goods they needed, everything requisite for developing new missions became at first difficult, and then impossible, to buy. The result was that for each mission Fr. Lasuén founded he had to beg for supplies from missions already established. Food was plentiful, but church goods, metal tools, and even soldier guards, for example, were in very short supply. Fr. Lasuén's really great achievement of founding four missions in about six months in 1797 was made all the harder by such scarcities.

Succeeding Fr. Serra as president of all the missions in 1784, Fr. Lasuén made it his first order of business to found Mission Santa Barbara, which Governor Neve had refused to allow Fr. Serra to do in April, 1782. With the consent, indeed the help of the new governor, Pedro Fages, the foundation ceremonies were performed on December 4, 1786.

Mission Santa Barbara soon attracted large numbers of Chumash Indian neophytes who labored in the construction of its first stone church. The violent earthquake of 1812 completely wrecked this church, but it was rebuilt in eight years. A later earthquake, in 1925, damaged this structure badly enough to require two years of restoration. The present church, with its majestic twin towers, seems to have been modeled on designs found in Vitruvius' Roman book on architecture.

By the secularization law of 1834, decreed by a newly independent Mexico, Mission Santa Barbara lost all its lands. Nevertheless, its buildings became the headquarters not only for Father Narcisco Durán, then president of the California missions, but also for Bishop Francisco Diego, California's first bishop. The United States made California one of its territories just in time to prevent outright private sale of all the mission's buildings by the voracious California governor, Pio Pico. In this way Santa Barbara became the only mission occupied continuously by Franciscans from the time of its founding down to the present.

To house its magnificent collection of books connected with mission history spacious archives have been built at Santa Barbara. For many years the archivist has been Fr. Maynard Geiger O.F.M., himself a celebrated Franciscan historian.

During the annual Fiesta Week crowds of Mexican-Americans make the mission church the center of their celebrations. And throughout the year both townspeople and visitors in large numbers come to the Masses there.

La Purísima Concepción

The site chosen for this mission lay only a few miles northwest of Santa Barbara, but preparations for its founding cost Fr. Lasuén a year of labor. At last he was ready to dedicate it, and did so on December 8, 1787, making it the third and last of the long hoped for Channel missions.

The first site was near the center of the present town of Lompoc. Mission Purísima, as it came to be called, prospered at first and completed its church in 1802. But here too the severe earthquake of 1812 reduced all its buildings to rubble. Fr. Mariano Payeras then moved the mission bag and baggage some four miles to the northeast, to the pleasant valley of Los Berros, and there rebuilt it.

Mission Purisima flouished until 1824, when the flogging of a Purisima neophyte by a corporal at Mission Santa Inés led to an uprising of the Indians at not only these two missions but at Santa Barbara also. The rebels at Purisima barricaded themselves in the church, with Fr. Antonio Rodríguez as hostage. They were, however, soon overrun by a Spanish force led by Lt. Estrada. Punishment was swift but would have amounted only to prison terms for the revolt's leaders had not seven of them in their excitement murdered four travelers coming down El Camino Real. These seven were hanged by the Spanish soldiers. In the end, almost all the neophytes returned to their home missions rather than flee into the dubious freedom of the hills.

Normalcy returned, to be broken again in 1834 by the law secularizing all mission lands. As for many other missions the results were catastrophic for Mission Purisima. It was gradually abandoned by neophytes and priests alike, who did not return even after the United States gave the mission back to the Church.

In 1934 five hundred acres of former mission land were bought by the County of Santa Barbara and became a state park. After careful research the mission compound was reconstructed by the Civilian Conservation Corps according to its original plans. Today the resurrected mission is an impressive establishment, much visited by travelers and also by groups of children from schools of the area.

Santa Cruz

Ever since the first Portolá expedition in 1769, the region at the northern end of Monterey Bay had been regarded by Franciscan explorers as highly suitable for a mission. It had water in plenty, timber of varying sizes, many acres of fertile land, and access to the sea. Its strategic location, besides, led the military authorities both in Mexico and in California to desire a mission there. So Fr. Lasuén had not merely official approval but express command when he founded Mission Santa Cruz on August 28, 1791.

But hardly had the mission started developing through the usual stages of winning converts and then building a church and its necessary adjuncts of livestock pens, granaries, and carpenter shops, when in 1797 an entirely unexpected town began to take shape not much more than a stone's throw away. Villa Branciforte, as it was called, consisted of settlers from the dregs of Mexican society who soon gave themselves over to their customary occupations of drinking, gambling, and prostitution.

Priests at the mission could not keep their neophytes away by persuasion from vices so conveniently close at hand. And when they resorted to punishments the neophytes either ran away or refused to listen to Christian instruction. The law which secularized the mission in 1834 completed the debacle.

In 1840, when only about 100 neophytes remained, an earthquake and tidal wave partially destroyed the mission buildings. By 1851 these structures had collapsed altogether. At other times and places an effort at rebuilding might have been made. But the morale, and probably the health, of the few remaining Indians were not up to the work. Instead, they carried away for other uses the mission's beams, tiles, stones, equipment of all sorts, and indeed anything usable left in the ruins.

Recently a replica, only half size, of the church and part of a cloister wing have been rebuilt after study of the original specifications.

Nuestra Señora de la Soledad

If the history of Mission Santa Cruz is tragic, that of Mission Soledad is at least equally so. Its troubles began on the day of its founding, October 9, 1791, when Fr. Lasuén had as one of his helpers a priest named Mariano Rubí, together with Fr. Diego García. As was customary, Fr. Lasuén left behind him these two founding priests to develop the new mission after he himself left. By making life intolerable for Fr. García, Fr. Rubí persuaded him to request a transfer, and in his place received Fr. Bartolomeo Gilí.

Fr. Rubí and Fr. Gilí had been comrades in mischief even at the College of San Fernando and should never have been sent as missionaries to California. They lacked any serious sense of vocation. At Mission Soledad they quickly won a scandalous reputation for their outrageous behavior and their constant complaints about everything and nothing. Not for them the careful religious instruction of their neophytes, or any other useful work.

They did not even replace with an adobe structure the brushwood shelter in which the mission had been dedicated. Both men had to be sent back to Mexico by Fr. Lasuén in 1793–1794.

By divine Providence their successor was Fr. Florencio Ibáñez, a faithful priest who served the mission well for fifteen long years until he died and was buried there. His grave lies near that of his friend, Governor Joseph Arrilaga, who came there to die with him. The mission's last priest was the holy and noble Fr. Vicente Francisco de Sarría, who carried on its work for the Indian neophytes until his own death in May, 1835, when his starved body was discovered at the foot of the altar.

Not the least of the griefs of Fr. Ibáñez and Fr. Sarría was the small number of neophytes at Soledad. A mysterious and severe epidemic in 1802 decimated them and made many potential new ones afraid to come.

When secularized in 1834, Mission Soledad's few possessions were moved to Mission San Antonio, and Soledad was abandoned. Since no stone building had ever been erected, its adobe structures soon collapsed into heaps of mud. Recent rebuilding so far has reconstructed the old chapel, as well as one side of the quadrangle. Although the original church washed away in a flood, its tile floor remains unharmed.

San José de Guadalupe

When Fr. Lasuén founded Mission San José on June 11, 1797, he did not have to beg Viceroy Branciforte and Governor Borica for permission, as in the old days. Quite the contrary. Taking the initiative themselves, these officials were demanding from Fr. Lasuén and his College of San Fernando at least five new missions as soon as possible in order to fill the gaps in the mission chain. These new establishments were to perform the double duty of strengthening California both against intrusions by foreign ships embroiled in the Napoleonic wars, and also against hostile Indian tribes still living unconverted in the central valleys.

Mission San José, for that reason, was placed where it commanded a major pass from the San Joaquin Valley, through which Indians from the interior could and did descend upon the Spanish coastal settlements to rob and slay. Consequently, it was really half presidio, half mission.

Needless to add that under these circumstances Christianizing these Indians was anything but easy. Nevertheless, Fr. Narciso Durán and Fr. Buenaventura Fortuni, both appointed to the mission in 1806 and both highly dedicated priests, labored there side by side for some twenty years with only moderate success. In 1833, after Mexico had won independence from Spain, the Mexican Governor Figueroa replaced Spanish Franciscans in the more northerly missions with others of the same Order trained in Zacatecas, who were natives of Mexico. Thus displaced, Fr. Durán retired to Mission Santa Barbara. His going spared him from having to watch the secularization of his former mission in 1836, which put it into the corrupt hands of the Vallejo brothers. They seized its lands and livestock for themselves.

An attempt by Pio Pico to sell the little that was left of the mission to his brother Andreas for pennies in 1846 was voided later by the United States government, which returned 28 acres to the Roman Catholic Church after California joined the Union.

Today all the mission's original buildings have vanished. The mission's adobe church was pulled down in 1868. In its place stands a white frame church. A small section of the original priest's rooms, with their porch, has survived. Restoration is in progress.

San Juan Bautista

This, the second of the four missions which Fr. Lasuén founded in 1797, he established on June 24. The almost miraculous speed with which he was moving is evident from the fact that he had founded Mission San José only eleven days earlier. He chose for the new Mission San Juan Bautista a site on the Río Pájaro because he judged that potential Indian converts abounded there.

And he was right. Three years later Mission San Juan Bautista had over 800 converts. By 1803 their numbers had increased so rapidly as to suggest that the church about to be built should be commodious. In 1808 Fr. Arroyo de la Cuesta, a newly arrived priest with spacious ideas, proposed that, in order to be roomy enough for all, the church should have not the usual single nave but three naves. His proposal was unfortunately accepted. When completed in 1812, the church did indeed have three naves, making it probably the largest in all the California missions. But the irony of it was that by this time the number of converts had decreased by half. Undaunted, Fr. De la Cuesta walled off the two outer naves from the central one except for apertures near the altar.

The unusual architecture seems to have made the walls especially vulnerable to earth tremors. Collapses and repairs seem to go on and on. Fr. De la Cuesta, however, remained proud of his church. Wanting to beautify its interior with mural paintings, in 1820 he hired an American sailor named Thomas Doak, who had jumped ship, to do the work. Meanwhile, being himself a gifted linguist who knew more than a dozen Indian languages, he spent his spare time writing two valuable books about them.

His colleague from 1812 on, Fr. Estevan Tapis, was also a gifted man with a real talent for music. He trained the neophytes in this art until his death in 1825, and he did not live long enough to be supplanted by the Zacatecans who took over the mission in 1833. But Fr. De la Cuesta did. He retired to Mission San Miguel, where he died in 1840.

Secularization caused Mission San Juan Bautista to lose all its lands. A fraction of these were restored, however, when President Buchanan gave the mission back to the Roman Catholic Church in 1859. The following year, an incongruous wooden bell tower was added to the mission church (as at San Luis Obispo), not to be torn down until 1950. The earthquake which nearly ruined San Francisco in 1906 also did extensive damage to the church at San Juan Bautista, though not to its convento.

At present, restoration is again in process, and Fr. De la Cuesta's walling off of the two side naves is being undone. The mission grounds are now extensively used for a retreat house.

As at Mission Sonoma the plaza next to the church was bought by the State of California in 1933, and its various buildings, including a hotel, have been made to look as they did during Gold Rush days. It is quaint but not too much so.

San Miguel Arcángel

Maintaining his dizzy speed, Fr. Lasuén dedicated Mission San Miguel on July 25, 1797, only a month after founding Mission San Juan Bautista. The veteran priest, Fr. Buenaventura Sitjar, who had recommended its site to Fr. Lasuén, became its first pastor, with Fr. Antonio de la Concepción Horra as his assistant. Within a few weeks the latter went insane and had to be sent back by Fr. Lasuén to Mexico City in hope of a recovery. He never recovered.

The native Salinan Indians who came to witness the mission's dedication ceremonies suffered no such tragedies. On the day of its founding they offered fifteen of their children for baptism, and many adults remained at the mission to learn the Faith. By the end of 1797 they completed a large stockade and built both a chapel and big adobe house. In the next year they constructed a larger church and a complex irrigation system to bring water to their fields from the Salinas River nearby.

All at the mission suffered a discouraging setback in 1806 when a fire consumed half the church roof and almost all their stocks of food. Under the direction of Fr. Juan Martín, pastor at the mission for twenty years, they not only rebuilt the burned out buildings but went on to build many new ones, such as a tannery, grist mill and granary, and a weaving room. Between 1816 and 1818 they erected the present great church, hauling timber from what is now Cambria, forty miles away on the coast. Finally, in 1823, the artist Esteban Muras taught the neophytes how to paint frescoes on the church's interior walls.

Before secularization in 1834 Mission San Miguel served the same double function as did Mission San José, though in a lesser degree keeping in check the hostile tribes of the interior while at the same time converting local people to Christianity. In 1816 Fr. Martínez of Mission San Luis Obispo and in 1818 Fr. Juan Cabot of Mission San Miguel accompanied military expeditions into the Tulare country to look for possible new mission sites. They found the native tribes quite uninterested in becoming Christians.

In those prosperous years Mission San Miguel had *asistencias* extending north and south for fifty miles and westward to the coast for forty miles to what is now called San Simeon, a village near the Hearst castle. The country around the mission itself is as hot and dry as a desert. But in these farflung *asistencias* it ran sheep and horses, cultivated barley, wheat, a small vineyard, and at San Simeon cattle and horses.

As usual, secularization blighted all these enterprises. In 1841 only Fr. Ramón Abella and some thirty neophytes still clung to the mission. But in 1846 the omnipresent Pio Pico sold all its lands to two buyers for $600. Thereafter, its convento wing was divided up into stores, one of them a popular saloon.

The United States government returned a part of the mission lands to the Roman Catholic Church in 1878, and in 1928 the Franciscans came back to occupy them. Since then, extensive restoration of the church and other buildings has taken place. Its mural paintings and ceiling decorations, however, remain untouched. Masses are now regularly said.

San Fernando Rey de España

Its founding on September 8, 1797, six weeks after that of Mission San Miguel, was the fourth and last of Fr. Lasuén's achievements in that year. Two months later, Mission San Fernando had forty neophytes and had completed a small church. Even today its permanent church building is a little smaller and narrower than the churches of the other missions.

The nearness of Mission San Fernando to the growing pueblo of Los Angeles did much to influence its development. By 1806 the mission was producing hides, tallow, soap, cloth, and other products much in demand in the pueblo. At the height of its fortunes San Fernando owned 13,000 cattle, 8,000 sheep, 2,300 horses—far more than its own needs dictated. It also had lengthened its convento so often to accommodate travelers on the way to and from the pueblo as to make it known far and wide as the "long building."

Troubles multiplied after 1811. The mission's neophyte population declined, no doubt because of the attractions of Los Angeles. The widespread 1812 earthquake made much rebuilding essential. Not least, the priests were fighting a losing battle with a continual seepage of settlers from Los Angeles on the mission's broad acres.

Then, too, there were the political problems. Having won its independence from Spain in 1822, the Mexican government, through Governor Echeandia, demanded in 1827, that Fr. Ibarra, the mission's pastor, renounce his allegiance to Spain. This he refused to do. Moreover, when the secularization law came into effect in 1835, Fr. Ibarra simply left Mission San Fernando Rey de España rather than see it devoured by the wolves bred by that process. Consequently he missed the transactions through which the omnivorous Pio Pico leased all the mission's lands to his brother Andreas. By 1888 its buildings were being used as a warehouse and a stable. Later, the mission grounds and patio became a hog farm.

Recovery began in 1896 when the Landmarks Club launched a campaign to reclaim the mission lands. In 1923 the Roman Catholic Church resumed possession, turning the mission over to Oblate Fathers. Restoration work suffered a setback in 1971, when an earthquake destroyed the church and part of the convento. Both buildings have now been restored.

San Luis Rey de Francia

This mission, founded by Fr. Lasuén on June 13, 1798, was the last of the five demanded of him by viceroy and governor and, indeed, the last he was ever to found before his death in 1803. Under the care of Fr. Antonio Peyri, its pastor for 33 years, it became the largest and most populous of all the missions. Indians thronged to become neophytes and received training in many practical industries. In fact, so many came that he found it necessary to establish a sub-mission at Pala with a chapel.

At its height Mission San Luis Rey had some 27,000 cattle and 26,000 sheep, not to mention vineyards and many orchards of olive and orange trees. To maintain all these a complicated aqueduct system had to be built, which also created pools for baths and laundries.

Seeing the coming of secularization, and powerless to stop the overthrow of all his work, Fr. Peyri took ship for Spain in 1832 despite the tears and pleadings of the Indian neophytes, who loved him. As usual the infamous Pio Pico divided the mission properties among his relatives and friends, not forgetting to take title, for himself and his brother, to some 90,000 acres of its lands. By 1846 San Luis Rey had ceased to be a mission; but attempts to sell the church itself were frustrated by John Frémont, acting for the United States government.

However, nothing could prevent the seizure of lands already partitioned out to the Indian converts. In 1903 those who survived were settled by the United States in a reservation at Pala. It is there that the best examples of Indian mural painting are still to be seen.

In 1861 President Lincoln had returned to the Catholic Church some 65 acres of the lands of Mission San Luis Rey. But not until 1892 did the Franciscan friars of Mexico occupy it to renovate the buildings and institute a novitiate. In 1893 the mission was rededicated, and renewed efforts at restoring it were begun by Fr. Joseph O'Keefe, who gave nineteen years to the work.

Today the mission church remains as it was in 1893, except that the roof has had to be replaced. It is now a Franciscan seminary.

Santa Inés

Shortly before his death in 1803 Fr. Lasuén sent Fr. Estévan Tapís to explore the hills behind Santa Barbara with a view to establishing a mission. In a broad, well-watered valley some 45 miles northeast of Santa Barbara, Fr. Tapis discovered and recommended what he considered to be a highly suitable site. Succeeding Fr. Lasuén as president of the California missions after the latter's death, Fr. Tapis lost no time in preparing to found a mission there. On September 17, 1804, he dedicated the present Mission Santa Inés (Agnes), watched by some 200 Indians, who offered 20 children for baptism on that same day. In spite of this favorable start, the neophyte population never exceeded 768. Perhaps others were frightened away by the insatiable 1812 earthquake, which reduced the church to rubble. Not until 1817 could a new church be built and dedicated.

With the help of an aqueduct bringing abundant water from the Santa Inés River the mission's field crops had increased rapidly by 1820. But in 1824 the progress of the mission suffered a setback. The mission's neophytes allowed themselves to be drawn into an uprising, in conjunction with those of Mission Purísima and Mission Santa Barbara. At Santa Inés, however, no armed confrontation with Lt. Estrada's forces occurred, as at Purísima. Santa Inés' Indian converts burned many buildings but worked to save the mission church when it was endangered by fire. News of Mexico's success in winning independence from Spain in 1822 perhaps helped to spark the abortive revolt.

By July, 1836, the mission had to endure the inevitable turmoil and robbery caused by the secularization laws. Its lands passed into the control of a civil administrator. Pio Pico could not lay his hands upon them, however, because between 1842 and 1845 the sympathetic Governor Micheltorena returned some 36,000 acres as a gift for the founding of a college of religious education. This college continued as an active seminary until 1882, when the Roman Catholic Church chose to sell most of its lands to private owners at a fair price.

The mission church at Santa Inés was never wholly abandoned. Hence restoration could begin early. Fr. Alexander Buckley worked at it from 1904 to 1930. About 1923 the Catholic Church placed the Capuchin Franciscan Friars in charge of the mission. In March, 1911, the bell wall of the mission church had been tumbled down by an earthquake. As at Mission San Luis Obispo, the bells were then placed in a wooden tower, which remained in operation until 1949. In that year William Randolph Hearst donated funds for tearing it down and replacing it with a solid concrete bell wall.

Today the tourist town of Solvang has expanded almost up to the mission's western boundary line, but unspoiled fields still stretch to the east and south. It is said that in a valley to the south remnants of a semi-Chumash village still exist.

San Rafael Arcángel

By 1817 so many of the Indians at Mission San Francisco de Asís (Dolores) had sickened and died in its cold and foggy climate that the possibility of building a hospital *asistencia* in the sunny valleys north of San Francisco Bay came under discussion. Father Prefect Sarría at first opposed the idea, but gave way when Fr. Gil y Taboada, famous for his knowledge of medicine, offered to go and take charge.

So on December 14, 1817, he founded his sanatarium. With the sick from Dolores and additional converts he had 300 neophytes at the end of the first year. For them he had erected a single plain building about 40 feet wide by 90 feet long, divided off into a chapel, a hospital, storerooms, and priests' quarters. By the end of 1819, having put matters into good order, he left the *asistencia* to Fr. Juan Amora. Actively seeking converts from the surrounding tribes, the latter soon had approximately 1,000 neophytes. In recognition of this achievement he was allowed to dedicate Mission San Rafael as an independent mission in its own right on October 19, 1822. The next year brought him into angry conflict with Fr.

Altimira, who proposed abolition of both Mission Dolores and Mission San Rafael and the assignment of all their converts to a new mission which he planned to establish farther north in Sonoma.

The harried Fr. Sarría finally managed to bring all parties to agree that Mission Dolores and Mission San Rafael were not to be abolished but that a third, a new mission in Sonoma, could be founded. Through all this hullabaloo Fr. Amorós continued to develop Mission San Rafael, enlarging its herds of livestock and bringing new fields under cultivation. He died in 1832, having served at San Rafael for thirteen years.

Shortly thereafter the mission was transferred to the Zacatecan Franciscans, represented by the formidable Fr. José Mercado. He strongly resisted attempts by General Mariano Vallejo, commander of the San Francisco Presidio to influence policies at San Rafael. Fr. Mercado laid himself wide open to charges of cruelty by arming and organizing his neophytes, and with them attacking villages of unconverted Indians, killing many. At the request of General Vallejo he was removed from his mission by Governor Figueroa.

Soon afterwards Mission San Rafael was secularized. And who should be appointed administrator of all its resources but General Vallejo? He immediately transferred all the mission's cattle to his own ranchos, together with equipment of every kind, all supplies, and even vines and fruit trees.

Mission San Rafael remained almost forgotten until 1909 when the Native Sons of the Golden West placed a mission bell at its approximate site. Recently a new building has been erected.

San Francisco de Solano

In his scheme to abolish both Mission Dolores and Mission San Rafael and to combine their resources in a new mission farther north, Fr. José Altimira actually had the approval of Governor Arguello, who saw such a mission as a barrier against the Russian garrison at Fort Ross if it should try to move southward. The brash young priest explored until he found a suitable site on July 4, 1823. He raised a cross there but made no attempt to found a mission until he could bring up his neophytes and necessary supplies from San Francisco.

Fr. Altimira managed to persuade some 700 neophytes from Mission Dolores to follow him north but had little luck in begging supplies from other missions, his only source of aid. They did not like his methods, and gave him only some livestock. For one reason or another the Russians at Fort Ross were far more generous, giving him bells and many sorts of equipment and supplies. Having these things in hand, he formally dedicated Mission San Francisco de Solano in April, 1824, and erected a completely wooden church.

Fr. Altimira did not understand how to handle his Indian neophytes. Many of them drifted back to their villages. Frustrated and angry, after persevering for only two years, he applied successfully in 1826 for a transfer to Mission San Buenaventura, far to the south. A few years later he smuggled himself out of the territory on an American ship.

Spanish Franciscans retained Mission San Francisco de Solano for seven years after Fr. Altimira left. In 1833 the Zacatecan Franciscans took it over under Fr. José Gutiérrez, whose discipline of his converts too often included the use of his whip. When secularization came in 1834, General Vallejo with his usual tactics simply seized the mission's goods and distributed them among his own ranchos.

These did not include the mission church. The town of Sonoma, begun in 1834, used it as a parish church until 1880. In that year most of the mission's few remaining possessions were sold, and the proceeds used to build a "modern little church" for the town. The already much decayed mission buildings continued to decay until bought by the State as a California State Landmark in 1910. They now form part of the town's public plaza. Like the plaza at Mission San Juan Bautista, it has been restored to look as it did a hundred years ago. In Sonoma, however, the mission church has been stripped of its religious features, which have been replaced by a museum display.

Appendix II
Table of the Franciscan Missions of California

The table which follows presents, at a glance, a synopsis of the history of all the Franciscan Missions of California and supplies other desirable information concerning them. The missions are listed in the order of their founding. Mentioned also are three stations attended from as many missions: the two Spanish settlements of Monterey and Los Angeles and the Indian sub-mission of Pala. Perhaps the most striking fact indicated is the total of the column captioned "Converts": the total number of Christian Indians who dwelt at the missions during the entire mission period is 89,663. Not all of these, of course, were converts from paganism; some were the children of such converts.

A closer examination of the Table, column by column, reveals the following facts: All of the 21 missions, except one, have been restored at least to some extent or a replica of some kind has been built; San Rafael is the only one of which nothing remained until recently. The oldest existing mission structure is the Serra Chapel at San Juan Capistrano, constructed in 1776-1785. Nine of the missions were founded by Father Serra, and nine by his successor, Father Lasuén; each of the remaining three were established by a different father. With a total of 7,854, San Gabriel had more Christian Indians during the whole mission period than any of the other missions. However, the mission which had the largest Indian population at any one time was San Luis Rey, where 2,869 Christian Indians dwelt in 1826.

The sites of the missions, including the three stations, are in 14 different counties of the state of California as follows: 4 in Monterey Co.; 3 in Los Angeles Co.; 3 in San Diego Co.; 3 in Santa Barbara Co.; 2 in San Luis Obispo Co.; and one in each of the 9 counties of Alameda, Marin, Orange, San Benito, San Francisco, Santa Clara, Santa Cruz, Sonoma, and Ventura. Thus most of the counties in which they are situated are likewise named for the missions.

The 21 missions and 3 stations are located in 4 Catholic dioceses: 8 in the archdiocese of Los Angeles; 8 in the diocese of Monterey; 5 in the archdiocese of San Francisco; and 3 in the diocese of San Diego. They are in the care of religious and secular priests as follows: diocesan clergy, 12; Franciscans, 4; Claretians, 2; Capuchins, 1; Jesuits, 1; Oblates, 1; Sons of the Sacred Heart, 1; and one is a museum and another a state park.

It is of interest to add that during the Spanish regime the missions had their highest population in 1806, at which time 20,355 Christian Indians were living at the 19 missions then in existence. During the Mexican regime, the 21 missions had a maximum population of 21,066 in 1824.

Noteworthy also is the fact that, even after the secularization of the missions, the Franciscans continued for some time to minister to the Indians as best they could. For instance, they remained at San Gabriel till 1834; at Soledad, till 1839; at San Luis Obispo and San Miguel, till 1841; at San Antonio and Santa Cruz, till 1844; at Purísima and San José, till 1845; at San Diego, till 1846; at San Fernando, till 1847; at San Juan Capistrano, till 1850; at San Juan Bautista, till 1854. But the only mission at which they have remained without interruption down to the present day is that of Santa Barbara.

The order of the missions according to their location on the *Camino Real* from south to north is as follows:

1. San Diego
2. San Luis Rey
3. San Juan Capistrano
4. San Gabriel
5. San Fernando
6. San Buenaventura
7. Santa Barbara

8. Santa Inez
9. Purísima Concepción
10. San Luis Obispo
11. San Miguel
12. San Antonio
13. Nuestra Señora de la Soledad
14. San Carlos
15. San Juan Bautista
16. Santa Cruz
17. Santa Clara
18. San José
19. San Francisco
20. San Rafael
21. San Francisco Solano

THE FRANCISCAN MISSIONS
OF CALIFORNIA

Mission	Founded	Present Church	Founder	Converts
1. San Diego	July 16, 1769	1813	Fr. Serra	6,638
2. San Carlos (Carmel)	June 3, 1770	1793-1797	Fr. Serra	3,957
2a. San Carlos (Monterey)	1771	1793	Fr. Serra	
3. San Antonio	July 14, 1771	1813	Fr. Serra	4,456
4. San Gabriel	Sept. 8, 1771	1795-1804/5	Fr. Serra (abs.) Fr. Somera	7,854
4a. N.S. de los Angeles	1784	1811-1822	Fr. Payeras (dedicated, 1822)	
5. San Luis Obispo	Sept. 1, 1772	c.1800	Fr. Serra	2,657
6. San Francisco (Dolores)	1776 (June 29-Oct.4)	1782-1791	Fr. Serra (abs.) Fr. Palóu	6,998
7. San Juan Capistrano	Nov. 1, 1776	1776-1777 & 1783-1785	Fr. Serra	4,404
8. Santa Clara	Jan. 12, 1777	1822 (replica)	Fr. Serra (abs.) Fr. Peña	8,640
9. San Buenaventura	March 31, 1782	1809	Fr. Serra	3,924
10. Santa Barbara	Dec. 4, 1786	1815-1820	Fr. Lasuén	5,679
11. La Purísima Concepción	Dec. 8, 1787	1816	Fr. Lasuén	3,314
12. Santa Cruz	Aug. 28, 1791	(small replica)	Fr. Lausén	2,466
13. N.S. de la Soledad	Oct. 9, 1791	(church rebuilt)	Fr. Lasuén	2,222
14. San José	June 11, 1797	1809 (part of mission)	Fr. Lasuén	6,737
15. San Juan Bautista	June 24, 1797	1803-1812	Fr. Lasuén	4,100
16. San Miguel	July 25, 1797	1812	Fr. Lasuén	2,588
17. San Fernando	Sept. 8, 1797	1806	Fr. Lasuén	2,839
18. San Luis Rey	June 13, 1798	1811-1815	Fr. Lasuén	5,591
18a. San Antonio de Pala	1822	1822	Fr. Payeras (dedicated, 1822)	
19. Santa Inez	Sept. 17, 1804	1814-1817	Fr. Tapis	1,411
20. San Rafael	Dec. 14, 1817	(nothing remains of mission)	Fr. Sarría	1,873
21. San Francisco Solano	July 4, 1823	1823	Fr. Altimira	1,315

THE FRANCISCAN MISSIONS
OF CALIFORNIA

Maximum Pop.	County	Diocese	In Care of	Address
1,829 (1824)	San Diego	San Diego	Diocesan clergy	11005 Friars Rd. San Diego, Calif.
876 (1795)	Monterey	Monterey	Diocesan clergy	P.O. Box 2235 Carmel, Calif.
	Monterey	Monterey	Diocesan clergy	P.O. Box 1511 Monterey, Calif.
1,296 (1805)	Monterey	Monterey	Franciscans	Box 257 Jolon, Calif.
1,701 (1817)	Los Angeles	Los Angeles	Claretians	537 West Mission Dr. San Gabriel, Calif.
	Los Angeles	Los Angeles	Claretians	100 Sunset Blvd. Los Angeles, Calif.
832 (1804)	San Luis Obispo	Monterey	Diocesan clergy	P.O. Box 1483 San Luis Obispo, Calif.
1,252 (1820)	San Francisco	San Francisco	Diocesan clergy	3321 16th St. San Francisco, Calif.
1,361 (1812)	Orange	Los Angeles	Diocesan clergy	Old Mission San Juan Capistrano, Calif.
1,464 (1827)	Santa Clara	San Francisco	Jesuits	University of Santa Clara Santa Clara, Calif.
1,328 (1816)	Ventura	Los Angeles	Diocesan clergy	211 East Main St. Ventura, Calif.
1,792 (1803)	Santa Barbara	Los Angeles	Franciscans	Old Mission Santa Barbara, Calif.
1,520 (1804)	Santa Barbara	Los Angeles	State Park	Old Mission Lompoc, Calif.
523 (1796)	Santa Cruz	Monterey	Diocesan clergy	Holy Cross Church Santa Cruz, Calif.
638 (1805)	Monterey	Monterey	Diocesan clergy	P.O. Box 506 Soledad, Calif.
1,886 (1831)	Alameda	San Francisco	Diocesan clergy	P.O. Box 3274 San José Mission, Calif.
1,248 (1823)	San Benito	Monterey	Diocesan clergy	P.O. Box 62 San Juan Bautista, Calif.
1,076 (1814)	San Luis Obispo	Monterey	Franciscans	P.O. Box L San Miguel, Calif.
1,081 (1811)	Los Angeles	Los Angeles	Oblates	15151 Mission Blvd. San Fernando, Calif.
2,869 (1826)	San Diego	San Diego	Franciscans	Old Mission San Luis Rey, Calif.
	San Diego	San Diego	Sons of the Sacred Heart	P.O. Box 66 Pala, Calif.
768 (1816)	Santa Barbara	Los Angeles	Capuchins	Box WW Solvang, Calif.
1,140 (1828)	Marin	San Francisco	Diocesan clergy	P.O. Box 3274 San Rafael, Calif.
996 (1832)	Sonoma	San Francisco	Museum	Old Mission Sonoma, Calif.

Bibliography

Attwater, Donald. *Penguin Dictionary of Saints.* Penguin Books, 1965.

Berger, John A., *The Franciscan Missions of California,* New York; G. P. Putnam, 1941.

Bolton, Herbert Eugene. *Rim of Christendom: a Biography of Eusebio Francisco Kino.* New York: Russell & Russell, 1960.

Bolton, Herbert Eugene, ed. *Historical Memoirs of New California by Fray Francisco Palóu, O.F.M.* 4 vols. New York: Russell & Russell, 1966.

Vol. I: Fr. Palóu's narrative of events in Baja California in preparation for the advance into Alta California.

Vol. II: 1. Fr. Crespi's Diary of the First Portolá Land Expedition, July 14, 1769 to January 24, 1770.

2. Second Portolá Expedition; Founding of Monterey.

3. Fr. Crespi's Diary of Fages' Expedition to San Francisco Bay, March 1772.

4. Overland journey of Fr. Serra and Capt. Fages, Monterey to San Diego, summer 1772.

Vol. III: Part I.

1. Anza's Diary of Second Land Expedition to Alta California, 1775-76.

2. Lt. Moraga's Account of the Founding of San Francisco, June 1776.

Part II.

1. First Anza Expedition, 1774.

2. Governor Rivera's exploration of San Francisco Bay as reported by Fr. Palóu's Diary, late 1774.

Vol. IV: 1. Anza's founding of San Francisco presidio and search for mission sites, narrated in Fr. Pedro Font's Diary, 1776.

2. Lt. Moraga founds Mission Santa Clara, January 1777.

3. Captain Rivera's Land Expeditions.

4. Fr. Pedro Font's Diary of Second Anza Expedition.

Butler, Alban. *Lives of the Saints,* rev. and ed. Herbert Thurston, S. J. and Donald Attwater. 4. vols. New York: J. P. Kenedy & Sons, 1956.

Caughey, John W., *California* (2nd ed.), New York, Prentice Hall, 1953.

Chapman, Charles E., *The Founding of Spanish California 1687-1783,* New York: The Macmillan Co., 1916.

Chase, J. S. and C. F. Saunders. *The California Padres and Their Missions.* Boston: Houghton Mifflin, 1915.

Cleland, Robert Glass. *From Wilderness to Empire: a History of California 1542-1900.* New York: Alfred A. Knopf, 1949.

Costansó, Miguel. *Diario Historico de los Viajes al Mar y Tierra Hecho al Norte de la California, 1770.* Mexico, 1950.

Costansó, Miguel. *Narrative of the Portola Expedition of 1769-70,* ed. Frederick Teggert. Berkeley: University of California Press, 1910.

Crespi, Fr. Juan. *See* Bolton, *Historical Memoirs,* vol. II, chapters 10-17.

Engelhardt, Zephyrin, O.F.M. *Missions and Missionaries of California.* 2 vols. Mission Santa Barbara, 1930.

Fages, Pedro. *A Historical, Political and Natural Description of California.* 1775, tr. Herbert I. Priestly. Berkeley: University of California Press, 1937.

Geiger, Maynard, O.F.M. *The Life and Times of Fray Junípero Serra 1713-84.* 2 vols. Washington, D. C.: Academy of American Franciscan History, 1959.

Geiger, Maynard, O.F.M. *The Indians of Mission Santa Barbara in Paganism and Christianity.* Franciscan Fathers, 1960.

Goodman, Marian. *Missions of California.* Redwood City, Calif., 1962.

Habig, M. A., and F. B. Steck. *Man of Greatness: Father Junípero Serra.* Chicago: Franciscan Herald Press, 1963.

Kenneally, Finbar, tr. and ed. *Writings of Firmín Francisco de Lasuén.* 2 vols. Washington, D.C.: Academy of American Franciscan History, 1965.

King, Kenneth M. *Mission to Paradise. The Story of Junípero Serra and the Missions of California.* Bicentennial Edition. Chicago: Franciscan Herald Press, 1975.

Kocher, Paul H., *Mission San Luis Obispo de Tolosa,* 1772-1972, San Luis Obispo, Calif.: Blake Inc., 1972.

Kroeber, A. L. *Handbook of the Indians of California,* Berkeley, Calif. Book Co., Ltd., 1953.

Lasuén, Fr. Francisco de. *See* Kenneally.

Nordhoff, Walter. *Journey of the Flame,* N.Y.: The Literary Guild, 1933.

Palou, Fr. Francisco. *See* Bolton, *Historical Memoirs,* vols. III and IV.

Robinson, W. W. *The Story of San Luis Obispo County,* Los Angeles: Title Ins. & Trust Co., 1957, 1964.

Sanchez, Nellie Van De Grift, *Spanish and Indian Place Names in California.* San Francisco: A. M. Robertson, 1914.

Saunders, Charles F. & J. S. Chase. *The California Padres and Their Missions.* Boston: Houghton Mifflin Co., 1915.

Webb, Edith B. *Indian Life at the Old Missions.* Los Angeles: Warren F. Lewis, 1952.

Weber, Fr. Francis J. *The California Missions as Others Saw Them (1786-1842).* Los Angeles: Dawson's Book Shop, 1972.

Wright, Ralph B. ed. *California's Missions.* Los Angeles: The Sterling Press, 1950.

Index